The Indus Civilisation and Later

Madhusudan Mishra

SHIPRA

Rs. 995

ISBN: 978-81-7541-890-5

2026 PoD, Imp.

First Published in India in 2018

The Indus Civilisation and Later

Published by:
SHIPRA PUBLICATIONS
LG 18-19, Pankaj Central Market
I.P. Ext., Patparganj, Delhi 110092, India
11 47322068; 96500 28065, 98105 22367
info@shiprapublication.com
www.shiprapublication.com

Preface

The manuscript of the book was ready for the press in 2006, but it is going to be published in 2017. In the meanwhile, some new chapters have been added.

This is actually the second part of 'The early Indus civilisation' published earlier, though it is quite independent of the same. My research on the Indus texts has followed the same line. The sound-values of the signs have never changed, but the meanings have been attached to them suiting my gradual understanding of the culture. I am unfortunate to the extent that no honest comments from the scholars have come. I am fully conscious of the fact that the scholarly world is not innocent. It is envious.

What we like to call the Indus language is the ur-Sanskrit, the most primitive or the first human speech, the grandmother of the IE language. I have been led to discuss the origin of the human speech itself, because the language is an evolution within the evolution of man, a biological product. As the man came to possess mind after a considerable gap in the creation, grammar, the mind of the language, began to evolve in the language at the agglutinative stage.

The theory of the biological origin of language has to be revived and hotly discussed, which was abandoned long ago. The language is a biological product like a plant or an animal, and is as conscientious as a man in its behaviour. It surveys the whole history of a form in a moment and meets its needs immediately. All the forms of a verb in its history lie at the tip of its fingers, and it does not take time to turn jātā hā (goes) or jā-e-gā (will go) into gayā (went), which existed some time ago in its history, connected with a synonymous verb. The idea of śabda-brahma is a truth: a śabda is the Brahma.

By this stage of my research on the Indus texts, I have been able to discover the relevance of the field symbols which have intrigued the scholars so far. Because the language of the Indus texts is isolating typologically, the field symbols were invented to make the texts expressive. They are like the cartoons of the modern journalism. For example, if a text simply says: 'the river is flowing from the mountain', the field symbol of a tiger with a trough in the front suggests its turbulent flow of destructive nature, which can be controlled by strong embankment and dug out canals or reservoirs by its side. It may be said to be a sort of human interference in the delayed change over to the agglutinative stage in the language. Because the language does not change as rapidly as the civilisation, the field symbols serve as prop to express the hidden ideas. It becomes a commentary of the text which could comprise a whole paragraph.

I have travelled a long way in the study of the Indus texts. I gave sound-values to the majority of the signs, interpreted them step by step from their crude meanings to the sophisticated ideas, and have ultimately cracked the field symbols to their utter relevance. But I am sorry to say: boddhāro matsaragrastāḥ (those who know are suffering from envy). Their outright rejection is a safer way to avoid scholarly discussion.

Madhusudan Mishra

Contents

1
Introduction

It is the continuation of 'The early Indus civilisation', virtually being its second part. The reading of the texts follows the same line, having the picture of an evolving primitive human civilisation in mind.

I have travelled a long way in the research on the Indus language, culture and history. Although my findings are haphazard and, often, unconnected, they are the results of the same endeavour.

I had realised in the very beginning of my research (1996) that the language of the Indus texts is typologically at the isolating stage. Later (2006), I preferred to call it 'the ur-Sanskrit', because it proved to be the grandmother of the pre-hymn Vedic language. In the Indus inscriptions itself, it is seen proceeding towards the agglutinative stage. But the further reading of the texts has proved that the Indus society was very rapidly getting modernised and it was forced to exploit the language beyond its capacity. Some texts are not easy to comprehend only on account of this haste.

The referends of the monosyllabic words are getting drastically enlarged, because they are not restricted to the local surroundings and living beings. That is why, I have been forced to attach such meanings to the monosyllabic words as are not easily conceivable. Some of the Indus clauses and phrases reflect in the bisyllabic and polysyllabic words of the modern rustic dialects. In this way, some signs too have been identified with specific sound-values. We will see that the expression 'the hole on the wall' relates to many situations and conditions with slightly deviating meanings. It shows how the language goes from the concrete objects to the abstract ideas.

The people of the early Indus civilisation are still seen exploiting the gifts of nature, and these gifts too were not in small varieties. The

Maṇḍūka-hymn of the RV may be one of the earliest, which appears to refer to 7000 BC on astronomical grounds, but even that is not distantly visualised in the texts of the Indus inscriptions. Thus these Indus texts may belong to the beginning of the new stone age, though the dating of an event is not within my competence.

The Indian culture is what the Indians essentially are. The Indus Aryans migrated to the west as fully civilised and urbanised people, at the beginning of the inflexional stage of the ur-Sanskrit. They had carried with them the civil engineering of Harappa. Therefore, they became the discoverers and inventors in the modern age. They were more adventurous than the people who remained behind. These home-sick people did not materially rise much above the ground, although spiritually they flew very high. Whatever they attained materially has gone to the depth of the earth and their spiritual gains are higher up in the sky. Whatever they wrote is often incomprehensible to us. We also disbelieve whatever they have said.

These people of the old age have seen several civilisations, both native and acquired, in course of their long history. The Indian culture is the invisible soul in the body of the nation, and the civilisations have been its atirements from the childhood to the present age. The body of this nation is full of wounds and scars, but the soul is as robust as before. Its beliefs have been characterised by thesis, anti-thesis and synthesis.

The phonemes of our languages and the forms in which they have been represented are truly native. Even though they have considerably changed by this time, we have been able to read and understand them because neither the ancient nor the modern is exotic to each other. Others could not read and understand them because they are not native to this culture. The Indus numeral || for ra still reflects in Tamil ர for the same ra-syllable, and the Indus sign for va  is almost the same as the Brahmi 𑀯.

The name "Indus" itself is not appropriate for this culture and civilisation. This culture of India began to flourish on the bank of the river Sarasvatī at the time when it was not known by this name. As it was the isolating stage of the ur-Sanskrit, people simply observed: ṣa ra ṣa = It flows from the mountain and stops at the sea. Later, when the clause fossilised as sáras 'pond', which characterised the bed of the river from the point of its origin to the sea, it was called saras-vat-ī (abounding in ponds). Then it was the Vedic period. By 1900 BC, this river dried up, which was so mighty at the time of the composition of the RV. The civilisation preceding the Vedic was the Sarasvatī civilisation, on account of which the river Sarasvatī has been adored as the goddess of learning. Gaṅgā and Sindhu, which lay on its periphery, might have been known to the people of the Sarasvatī culture, but the names 'perennially going' for Gaṅgā and 'stealthily flowing' for Sindhu came much later. Gaṅgā from gam (to go) is not palatalised on the first syllable and is younger than the verbal form jagāma, and Sindhu from syand has aspiration on the second syllable and Samprasāraṇa on the first syllable.

The Gaṅgā, Sindhu and Sarasvatī are Vedic names. But Asikni, Vitastā, Puruṣṇī, Vipāśā and Śutudrī are ur-Sanskrit names. The Indus texts appear to suggest how these names came up later. 'The hole on the wall' is suggestive of the canals dug out from the main river. There is a chapter on the names of the rivers in this book.

The decipherment of the Indus texts will go on. Both the reading and interpretation are as difficult as the excavations of the Indus sites themselves. The rust of the phonetic decay has to be carefully cleansed and the intended meanings of the clause and phrases have to be seen microscopically. We are amused to see the Indus clauses and phrases squeezed and decayed into incomprehensible Vedic vocables, but their analysis put us on such a crossroad, where we find the genuine way.

The persons who laugh at this embarrassing job are not few, but they will ultimately realise the truth, because: kālo hyayaṃ nir-avadhir vipulā ca pṛthvī (the time has no limit, and the earth is vast).

By this time, however, I have been able to grasp the intention of the employment of the field symbols along with the texts. Because the language of the Indus texts is very primitive, the intelligent speakers of that language made it more expressive by employing the field symbols. They are the proto-types of the cartoons of the modern journalism.

Decoding of the Indus texts is an arduous task. First of all, the reading or the phonetic identification itself is full of uncertainties. If, however, it is achieved, the interpretation is more difficult. A pre-requisite for it is finding the fossil of the clause in the later language, ancient or modern. If the fossil is identified and its meaning is ascertained; it is to be expanded in the form of a clause and make it agree with the clause in question. The fossil is in the form of an adjective or noun, one lexical term, but it has to be divided into two ideas of subject and verb.

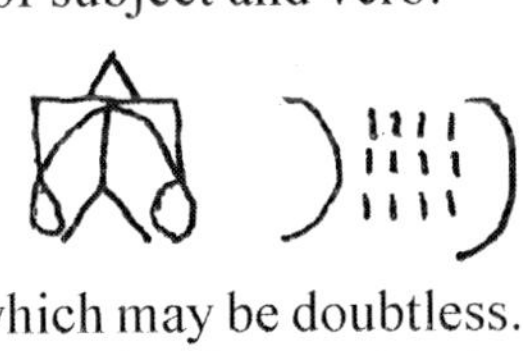

This text reads śiṭhi, which may be doubtless. This śiṭhi phonetically seems to reflect in the Vedic śiti adj. meaning 'white'. The compounds, of which it is the first member, qualify some creatures or animals. The dusky steeds of Savitṛ, for example, is called 'white-footed'.

At the isolating stage of the ur-Sanskrit, śiṭhi was a clause. In Vedic, it is an adjective. We cannot form any idea of this long gap of time. It may be a millennium. But the field symbol of a unicorn with a trough in front suggests some unfortunate event. The whiteness may be associated with snow or similar object. It is said that in the glacial age the avalanche from the polar region used to wipe out the countries on its path. If the clause recounts the event of an ancient period, the text seems to say: the avalanche rolled (southwards). This may be the basis of the meaning 'white' for śiti.

The Indus inscriptions are very old, and they recount the events of a more ancient period, told from generation to generation. The stories of the rolling avalanche would have been recounted by the old people to the new generation. This is one of them in recorded form. It seems to be a text of the ancient history.

2
The Biology and Psychology of the Human Speech

The animals walk horizontally. Therefore, their larynx is contiguous with their tongue. The sound produced in the larynx proceeds uninterruptedly through the tongue and comes out as the bellowing of the bull or buffalo, as the roaring of the lion or tiger, and as the long cry of the little animals. The length of the animals' cry is remarkable. In case of the monkeys, the length of noise is reduced, because they are much advanced in evolution.

When the cavemen began to walk erect, their larynx got away from the tongue and the continuity of noise broke down. The length of their utterance was sharply cut short. The first resonant, called vowel, was pieced as syllable, either with one mātrā when it was called short, or with two mātrās when it was called long. They also produced vowels with three mātrās when somebody was called from a distance. But when the same long vowels met in the living speech, they simply merged together as a long vowel, not as a vowel with three or four mātrās.

The early vowels produced by the human beings formed a triangle of a i and u in the diagram of the cardinal vowels: the low vowel a in the centre, and i u at the highest point in front and back. Later, i and u climbed down to e and o.

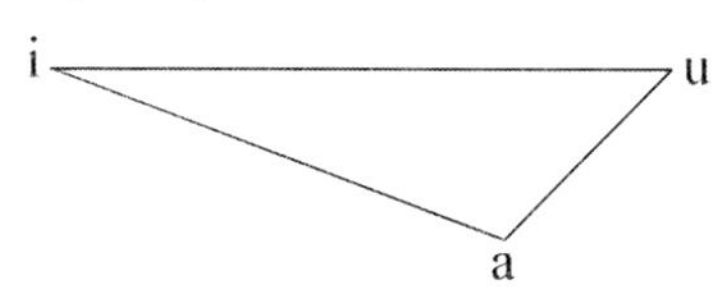

As a and ā combined with i and u, the diphthongs ai āi au āu came out. When i and u were immediately followed by different vowels, the tongue could not reach the required height for i and u, which turned into the fricative y and v respectively. Gradually, the other resonant called the breathing h, the trilled r, the lateral l as well as the nasals and sibilants were born. All these sounds were continuants. But when the tongue began to stop the breath-stream with its different parts for a moment and release it sharply, the stops or explosives were born. They were either voiceless or voiced.

They were also either plain or aspirated. Named after their places of utterance, they are: Velars k kh g gh; Palatals c ch j jh; Cerebrals ṭ ṭh ḍ ḍh; Dentals t th d dh; Labials p ph b bh (the breath-stream stopped by the lips). The palatals are either stops or affricates. Among the stops too, the plain voiced labial b was the first to be born. It is a dying sound in IE.

These vowels and consonants are human sounds, but some of these like h produced near the throat and m produced with nose are also common to men and animals. The human beings imitate the noise of the horse with h, of the cock with k, of the bull with m, and so on. If some human sounds appear to reflect in the sounds of the external objects, they become the basis of their identification and the syllables become the names of those objects. Therefore, ha means 'horse', ka means 'peacock', bha means 'bee' in the traditional Sanskrit lexicons of the monosyllabic words. Our lexicography is very old.

The speech is an evolution within the evolution of the human beings. I mean to say that the human speech is a biological product. Its status as such requires to be hotly discussed.

The early human beings started speaking monosyllabically. Initially, it was in the form of an order: ra = run away, ṭha = turn (to left or right), ha = stop, etc. This justifies the presence of single signs in the Indus texts. Ha is even now spoken to stop an animal.

They had come out from the caves and begun to identify their syllables with the beings and objects in the surrounding. They also began to draw their pictures as convenient to them. These pictures themselves became their early writings, and they stood for certain sounds referring to certain beings and objects. They pictographed a 'turtle' which they called ka, 'two horns of a bull' which they called ga, an 'ant' which they called ca, and so on. Gradually, the same syllable began to stand for other beings and objects without any clash of the referends. Thus, though ka stood for turtle among the reptiles, it also stood for peacock among the birds, and so on. The Indus texts portray a 'man' for ra, the 'hindleg of a horse' for la, a kind of 'fish' for na, 'another kind of fish' for ma, yet another kind of fish' for ha, a 'dog' for ḍha, a 'bee' for bha, a 'mountain' for da, the 'hood of a serpent' for pha, a 'bird' for sa, and so on. The basis of the identification of sound and meaning was physical but, gradually, through the association of ideas, even abstract feelings began to be expressed through the same sounds. Unfortunately, all beings and physical objects are not seen pictographed for the appropriate sounds.

The animal figures are seen gradually changing into the geometrical figures, so that the same syllables have two representations. Of course, not all syllables are seen represented by the geometrical figures.

At some height of their civilised social life, when they could know the qualities and the places of articulation of the sounds of their speech, they invented the numeral script, the strokes of different shapes and sizes increasing in number, which appear to reflect in the syllabic order of the Māheśvarasūtras[1] at the beginning of the Pāṇini's grammar. The following is the arranged order of the numerals from right to left:

10 9 8 7 6 5 4 3 2 1

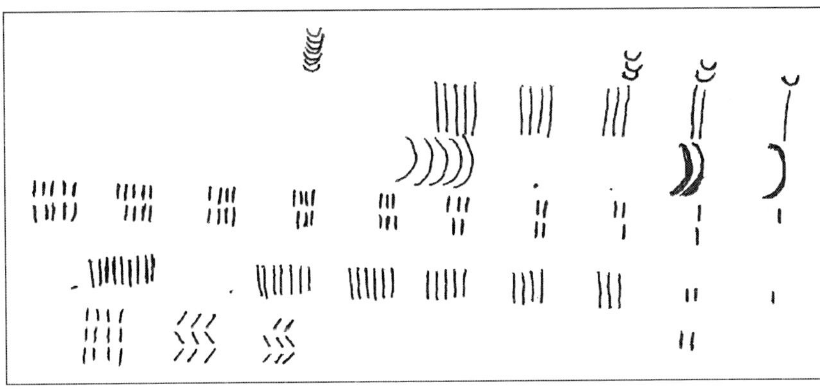

The first line represents the vowels, but it is incomplete and disturbed from the Sanskrit point of view: u i o....? Pānini had taken note of this order, although the Sanskrit order is: a i u etc.

The next line from the right represents the following syllables, Pāṇini reading them from left to right:

10	9	8	7	6	5	4	3	2	1
					ha	ya	va	ra	la
					ña	ma	ṅa	ṇa	na
jha	bha	gha	ḍha	dha	ja	ba	ga	ḍa	da
kha	pha	cha	ṭha	tha	ca	ṭa	ta	ka	pa
śa	ṣa	sa						ẖa	

Of course, some numeral signs are not represented in the list, though they can be reconstructed. In two cases the order has been exchanged by the Sanskrit school.

Because the Indus texts have been written with animal figures, geometrical figures and numerals alternately in the duplicate texts, almost

1. This nomenclature itself shows the hoary antiquity of this syllabic order. The time-reckoning system of the western scholars may go into coma.

all syllables, except a few, have been identified and read with definite sound values.

The extent texts of Indus represent the isolating stage of the language. The words are monosyllabic and there is no grammar. A single syllable is either an order or a verb in the indicative mood. In the two-syllabic texts, the first is the subject and the second is the verb. In the three-syllabic texts, it is either subject + object + verb or the oblique-case + subject + verb. The language moves instinctively like the early beings of the creation. A line may consist of one clause or two and many clauses:

ṇa ga = The light is going away
va ṇa ṣa = The water gives life
ta ṇa ṣa = From the womb gems come out
ṣa ra ṣa = From the mountain flows; stops

Though the first human cry was in the form of an order, the Indus texts show some examples of an order by adding -ga after a verb. The future tense too was shown by -gha added to a verb. The grammar had begun to appear in the language. It was now at the agglutinative stage.

Just as men came in possession of mind after considerable gap in evolution, the languages came to possess the mind in the form of grammar at the agglutinative stage. It came to maturity at the inflexional stage. The development of grammar in the language and the maturity of the human mind are synchronous. The language has the sound system as its body and the grammar as its mind. It has evolved like the human being.

But at the inflexional stage of the ur-Sanskrit the speakers began to migrate to foreign lands due to some natural disaster or want of space. Therefore, the reconstructed Indo-European was bound to be inflexional. It could not be reconstructed at the earlier stage of the language. It has, however, been reconstructed hyper-inflexionally, and the direction of the phonetic evolution has been lost. Therefore, impossible words have been reconstructed or created. Let us proceed with an imaginary ur-Sanskrit clause: gā (goes) va (into the stable); phrase - gāva (going into the stable); lexical term gāva (cattle, bull). The term gāvī was known to Patañjali. At the agglutinative stage, the pl. form was gāva-ṣa. At the inflexional stage it was reduced to gāvas due to accent on the first syllable. It was at this stage of the language that the speakers began to migrate to different countries. There were phonetic changes and morphological innovations at every station. The first syllable gā was reduced to cu in old English through the proto-Germanic go -. The final element -vas was adopted as bos in Latin. The original acc. pl. gās became calf and the Latin bos became beef, boef in old English through the Anglo-Norman sources. But all these forms are traced to the IE gwōus, which did not ever exist. Hirt had to say that one should not be concerned with what was spoken in IE.

The grammar being the mind of the language, the latter moves very conscientiously like an intelligent human being, eliminating the ambiguities even at the cost of regularity. Therefore, the Indian grammarians and philosophers have conceived the idea of a śabda-Brahma whose memory is excellent and the discretionary power is overwhelming.

Bloomfield's definition of the morpheme as 'a linguistic form that bears no partial phonetic-semantic resemblance to any other form' began to stagger on the second step. The pl. suffix -s has many alternants which are also irregular, sometimes zero, and also having minus features, which defeat the very idea that morphemes consist of phonemes. Frank Palmer states that 'morpheme features truly relate to the agglutinative language'. The inflexional stage has been reached after a long journey, and there was innovation at every milestone. A linguist, like a blind man describing an elephant by touching its different parts, gives various descriptions of the same form at different points of encounter. He ignores the fact that the language has a mind and an excellent memory. It knows its whole path from the beginning to the present stage. Hindi has the form jātā hä (he goes), jā-e-gā (he will go) from jānā, but for the past tense it goes back to Apabhraṃśa to fetch gayā from the kindred verbal form gata from gam 'to go'. Similarly, the take-took controversy can be settled by assuming 'took' to be a past form at some milestone on the way of its journey. Hockett's IA proposal suggests the right solution. It was there in the language. It is not newly created. A form never dies in the memory of the language.

In Aorist 3p 2p sg. middle, the Sanskrit verb kṛ 'to do' has very conscientiously guillotined the legitimate -s- (3. a-kṛ-ta 2. a-kṛ-thās) to evade any confusion with kṛṣ 'to draw', though elsewhere (d. a-kṛ-ṣ-ātām pl. a-kṛ-ṣ-ata) it has been retained.

The French verb devoir has circumflexed the past participle dû only to avoid confusion with du = de + le. The present participle from avoir is ayant, because the legitimate avant is already a word for 'before'.

The behaviour of different languages shows that they have a mind corresponding to the mental level of their speakers. It is like a living being, integrally attached to men. Though we cannot see it, we feel its existence.

The typological classification of languages as isolating, agglutinative and inflexional refers to the physical body of the languages, and their classification as analytic and synthetic refers to the existence of mind in it.

The term isolating should not be confused with the analytic. The analytic state is reached in the language after the inflexion begins to disappear. At the agglutinative stage the language acquires a mind in the form of grammar, which is fully mature at the inflexional stage. That is why, Sanskrit, Greek and Latin have produced excellent literature. The inflexional body of the language brings it in synthetic state, because a number of ideas are synthesised in a single form. Even when the inflexion dwindles and the language shows a downward slope, the mind of this naked Yogi becomes more acute. That is to say, the mind of the analytic language becomes wonderfully sharp and its whole history comes at the tip of its finger. It is at the analytic state of the language that the world has reached the dizzy heights in science and technology. The English language has exceeded all the languages of the world in the acuteness of mind.

The Sanskrit grammarians and philosophers have not only conceived the idea of a Śabda-Brahma but they have also referred to the wonderful śabda-śaktis called Abhidhā, Lakṣaṇā and Vyañjanā. The first power gives the meaning of the utterance at the material level, the second at some higher level and the third at the spiritual level.

Therefore, Swāmī Dayānanda had opined that the Vedic mantras have both material and spiritual meanings.

The RV 2, 4, 5 cd: sa citreṇa cikite raṃsu bhāsā jujurvāṃ yo muhur ā yuvābhūt literally means: He (Agni) was observed in ashes through his brilliant lustre who, even when grown old (= about to be extinguished), became young again.

Apart from the fact that it relates to some prehistoric event, what it wants to convey can be described in a whole paragraph:

The Agni represents the truth, which shines from inside. But often it is covered by the ashes of falsehood. Once these ashes are removed, the truth shines forth brightly. That is to say, the old Agni becomes young. The truth exposes the falsehood.

It is certain: the language has a mind, and it is as much a living being as a plant or an animal. Its body consists of words and meanings of the three types, which are themselves suggestive in each case. (Kāvya-prakāśa of Mammaṭa 2, 8). With the aid of mind in the form of grammar, the language expresses any idea precisely and unambiguously. However, when what is said is positive linguistically and negative intentionally, and vice versa, the linguistic analysis of the sentence becomes difficult. The linguistics is not competent to undertake this task. The mind of the language is as complex as the same of a human being. The language is a super-biological product.

B. Evolution of Meanings

Very long after the animal's cry turned into articulate human sounds, broken into syllables, all summarised in the syllabic order of the Māheśvarasūtras at the beginning of the Pāṇini's grammar, the primitive human beings began to identify the sounds of their speech with the similar sounds of the physical objects and beings in the surroundings. They observed that the peacocks produced the k sound, the horses produced the h sound, the serpent's hissing resembled their s sound, and so on. They hastened to name the peacock as ka, the horses as ha, the serpents as sa, and so on, The traditional Sanskrit lexicons of the monosyllabic words are seen to have associated phonemes with specific animals. We suppose that all syllables would have been the names of specific animals, birds, reptiles or other beings of the surrounding. The physical non-living objects too produce sounds identifiable with the phonemes of the human speech. For example, the rattling of the burning fire reflects in the trilled r of the human speech, a drum produces the ḍ sound, the tinkling of the bells is like the ṭ sound, and so on. Therefore, in the traditional lexicons of the monosyllabic words, ra means 'fire', ḍa means 'drum', etc. The activities too of these beings and objects reflect in the meanings of the monosyllabic words: ra means 'speed', that is, 'to run' on the basis of the rapid spreading of the fire in the forest, and so on.

Some animals and birds have bisyllabic names, obviously of later origin: a crow is called kāka, an elephant is called gaja, a goat is called aja, and so on. A goat would have been originally called just a. It is proved by the depiction of the 'horns of the goat on its head' for a in the Brahma alphabet (*see* p. 19), placed obliquely. In the rustic dialects of the countryside, some monosyllabic words still survive. For example, ṭa means 'leg', which suggests the meaning 'to walk'. This ṭa had the past form ā-ṭa (he walked) at the agglutinative stage of the ur-Sanskrit which, analysed as a-aṭ-a at the inflexional stage, gave birth to a new verb aṭ 'to walk'.

Gradually, all phonemes of the human speech began to stand for particular ideas, objects and beings of daily encounter in the surrounding, based on some reasonable choices of the speakers, scrupulously avoiding the clash of referends. Thus ka stood for a peacock alone among the birds, for a turtle alone among the reptiles, for the water alone among the liquids, and so on. Ha is even now spoken to stop an animal in the countryside. Its association with sky, having sound as its chief quality, gave it the meaning 'to speak'. Then ā-ha was its past form in the agglutinative stage of the ur-Sanskrit which, analysed as a-ah-a at the inflexional stage, gave birth to the verb ah, which disappeared very early in the history of the language.

It is true that the number of ideas or objects and beings is far greater than the phonemes of a language. Therefore, they have to be scrupulously distributed among them, one phoneme standing for specific ideas, objects and beings.

The origin of a language was an event beginning a hundred thousand years ago when, in the nomadic life of the people, a phoneme acquired a particular meaning, which also changed as they changed their habitation. Even after they had given up their nomadic habits and settled in villages, their changing way of life drastically changed the meaning of a phoneme. That is why, a 'turtle' is named sometimes a, sometimes ka, and sometimes ca.

It is said that the primitive people changed their vocabulary after every generation. Therefore, the same phoneme has different meanings in the different Ekākṣarakośas. The cerebral ṇa is once said to mean pāniya-nilaya 'residing in waters', which should naturally go to the 'fish sign' in the Indus script, standing for na, however.

The syllables themselves, 34 consonants × 14 vowels, amount to 476 in their ordinary forms. But, if ligatures are taken into account, 34 × 34 × 14, they may amount to more than 15000. Of course, this number is theoretical, but all the possible number of syllables may form a little pocket dictionary.

At least more than 400 syllables of this type are actually recorded in the texts of the Indus writings. Some others are attested by their use in the Tantric texts, though their meanings are sectarian and arbitrary. For example, sapta (= 7) is analysed as sa-pta meaning 'having matted hairs', said to be the name of Śiva.

It may be supposed that the individual syllables initially expressed an action, then a state. That is to say, the verb preceded the noun in the evolution of meaning. Of course, like the vowels, the pronouns were the first to emerge in the language: ī 'this', ū 'that', etc.

A simple monosyllabic word in the Indus texts may be an order: ra = run away!, ha = stop!, etc. As they penetrated the uncultivated areas in the countryside, they were frequently warned to be careful. Their field-symbols are more vocal in this respect.

There were also bisyllabic words by the combination of two syllables; na (flows) and da (makes indistinct noise) form na-da referring to a 'noisy river'. Some bisyllabic words cannot be analysed as to the value of the individual syllables: vi-ḍa means 'flat nose', because viḍ-āla 'flat-nosed' is the name of the 'cat'.

We have tata 'father' in the early Vedic language, but we cannot say how the repetition of ta signified 'father'. The ligatured monosyllabic words are hard nuts to crack. Though śrī 'beauty' and others are easy to understand in spite of their difficult analysis, dra and vra of the AV are still obscure.

Some three-syllabic clauses have various milestones in the development of their meanings. The clause ta na ṣa originally meant: from the mountain (ta) the river (na) flows (ṣa). In the settled life of the people, the same clause meant: from the reservoir (ta) canals (na) are dug out (ṣa). At a more advanced stage of their social life, it meant: from the womb of a woman (ta) gems (na) come out (ṣa). The fossilised form of this clause in the RV is tánas 'child'.

The monosyllabic words, and some bisyllabic words too, form the vocabulary of the isolating stage of the ur-Sanskrit. It was like the early creatures of the creation, full of life but moving instinctively. It had no grammar. There was an instinctive order of the subject, object and verb. The idea of the oblique cases evolved later, which was placed at the first position. The Indus texts represent the isolating stage of the ur-Sanskrit.

At the agglutinative stage, partly represented in the Indus texts, the grammar began to evolve. The past forms like ā-ha are not quotable, but there are future forms like ra-gha (it will shine) and the imperative forms like va-ga (irrigate!), etc. Though unquotable in the Indus texts, the monosyllabic verb ma (time) = 'to grow old' added the perfect affix -ha. We imagine a clause tata maha = the father has grown old. Later it fossilised as tatā-maha 'grandfather'. The monosyllabic verb ca 'to be, take place' added the pluperfect affix -ra. A possible clause ku cara is obscure as to its meaning. Even the fossilised adjective kucara is still obscure in the RV (1.154.2): mṛgo ṇa bhīmaḥ kucaro girṣṭhāḥ. Later, Pāṇini noted -maha in pitāmaha, mātāmaha, etc. (4.2.36), also the widely used -cara (5.3.53). He has also noted some fossilised verbal forms as secondary suffixes (5.2.24-33). Some bisyllabic words of the agglutinative stage of the ur-Sanskrit have transited into the Vedic. The word hi-ma (milk on the top of the mountain) = snow is one of many such words, traceable in the other IE dialects. But many of them have either disappeared or become obscure in meaning.

As the bisyllabic words were created at the agglutinative stage of the ur-Sanskrit, the monosyllabic words were becoming outdated and disappearing. At the fully mature stage of the ur-Sanskrit at the agglutinative stage, the monosyllabic words were completely ousted. The lexicographers began to compile them, but by this time it was too late. The underivable bisyllabic words of Sanskrit like aja (goat), gaja (elephant) are said to be of unknown etymology. They cannot be derived from the Vedic verbs. If we take the Vedic vocabulary back to the agglutinative stage of the ur-Sanskrit, no Vedic word can be said to be of unknown origin.

The traditional Indian commentators try to etymologise some words by giving meanings to individual syllables. Really they try to take the inflexional Sanskrit back to the agglutinative and isolating stage. Though they appear to be successful at many places, they are severely criticised by the modern etymologists.

An individual syllable was meaningful at the isolating stage of the ur-Sanskrit. It was carried upto some distance even at the agglutinative stage. But as the third syllable was added, the phoneme turned into morpheme and no trace of the original meaning was left. At the inflexional stage and on its downward slope towards the analytic state, a phoneme had only the capacity to differentiate meanings. That is to say, no phoneme of a language had any meaning. If two sounds appear to be dissimilar in a pair of words having the same meaning, the two sounds are the allophones of the same phoneme. On the other hand, two similar sounds in a pair of words having different meanings are two different phonemes.

Because the phonemes had ceased to be meaningful in extending the size of a word after the agglutinative stage and later, the extension of words began to be carried out by the process of compounding. Then two or more words were compounded and new meanings evolved. There are well-recognised classes of compounds in the Sanskrit language.

C. Reading the Indus Script

The speech of the primitive people consisted of full syllables, either vowels alone or consonants + vowels. The language of the Indus people, as represented in the Indus texts, belonged to the isolating stage in the typological classification of the languages: there was no grammar, and the words were monosyllabic. A particular order of syllables formed a small clause. It was the ur-Sanskrit, if named specifically.

The vowels, including the diphthongs, were the following:

a ā i ī u ū e ē o ō ai au āi āu = 14. The consonants were the following:

Fricatives	ha	ya	va	ra	la						
Nasals	ña	ma	ṅa	ṇa	na						
Voiced stops	jha	bha	gha	ḍha	dha	ja	ba	ga	ḍa	da	
Voiceless stops	cha	pha	kha	ṭha	tha	ca	ṭa	ta	ka	pa	
Sibilants	śa	sa	ṣa								
Breathing	<u>h</u>a										= 34

After several centuries, the same language transited into the agglutinative stage: grammar began to evolve gradually. The particular syllabic order began to be reinforced by the morphological elements. When the grammatical concepts were fully mature, expressed by the appropriate morphological elements, the language transited into the inflexional stage, which later evolved as the Vedic language.

Though the extant Indus texts truly represent the isolating stage of the ur-Sanskrit, some grammar had already begun to appear.

The 14 vowels and 34 consonants would have constituted $34 \times 14 + 14 = 490$ syllables, which would have been the total wealth of vocabulary of that primitive language.

As each syllable would have been the name of the animals, birds, reptiles and the remarkable non-living objects of the surrounding, the easiest of them could have been pictographed. They would have seen that their audible sounds had become visible. They could not only speak and hear their sounds, they could also see them. They hastened to draw them in the following way:

1		*2*		*3*		*4*		*5*	
ka (turtle)	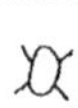	kha	–	ga (horn of a bull)		gha (neck)		na -	
ca (ant)		cha -		ja (bat)		jha (fish)		fla -	
ṭa -		ṭha (bearer)	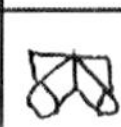	ḍa (drum)		ḍha (dog)		ṇa (man)	
ta (breast)		tha -	–	da (mountain)		dha (backbone)		na (fish)	
pa (leaf)		pha (hood of a serpent)		ba (spider)		bha (bee)		ma (fish)	
ya -		ra (runner		la (hindleg of a horse)		va (arrow)			
śa (hare)		sa (bird)	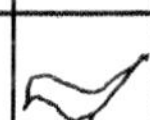	ṣa (nipple)	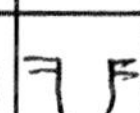	ha (fish)			
h̲a (unicorn)									

The variants of the animal signs show their evolution through time, as in case of ṭha and ṇa. The crude animal figures were also turning to be geometrical. The fish of several types were known to them by specific names. Thus there were four fish signs for jha, na, ma and ha.

Some syllables have no pictograph. The vowels are completely missing in the animal figures. But we suppose that there must have been the pictographs for a i u e o, if not also for the diphthongs.

It may be supposed that, initially, there would have been 490 or so many drawings for all the possible syllables, but finally the a-syllables were retained, others shown by some change in the original shapes. The variants in the animal figures probably show the different vowels after the consonants. For example, the 'ant' sign has six variants out of their seven occurrences. These variations must have been intentional.

In the Indus writing itself, there is a clause of subject + object + verb, exclusively in the animal figures:  ja  pha  śa (the hind-leg of a horse causes wound).

In course of time, the same syllables began to be written with the geometrical shapes, retaining however the animal figures, as far as possible. Each syllable came to have duplicate forms. But in one line the same syllable was rarely written in two ways. The geometrical figures, as far as recognisable, are the following:

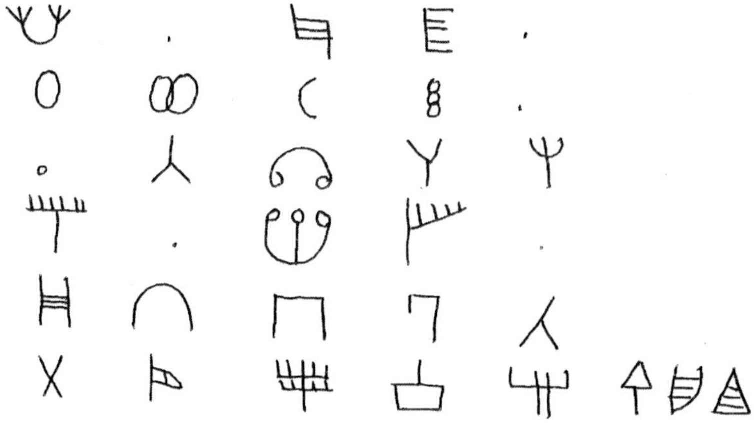

ka	kha	ga	gha	ṅa
ca	cha	ja	jha	ña
ṭa	ṭha	ḍa	ḍha	ṇa
ta	tha	da	dha	na
pa	pha	ba	bha	ma

ya ra la va

śa ṣa sa ha h̲a

It cannot be said what these symbols stood for in their primitive minds. For us, they are the arbitrary different drawings for the syllables.

The simple vowels appear to be identifiable among the geometrical figures (*see* page 18):

a ā i ī u ū e o

They also make some diphthongs:

rau rāu rai gāi raē haō

We can see how cleverly they have made the long vowels.

While some syllables are seen to have two forms, a few are still missing in the geometrical figures; kha and ṇa are not represented, while  and 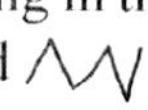 are not identifiable.

Some vowels are represented diacritically:

ru ri yu ṣu ṣi ṭhi

These little signs can be put anywhere as subscript:

Various forms of bracketing indicate the vowels:

rā ḍho ghî śi

There are some composite signs making ligatures:

ṣṭa ṣṭha ska kṣa ṣḳa

Some signs are identifiable due to their composite form.

Some signs appear to be the geometrical version of the animal figures:

ḍha da

The variants of the geometrical signs indicate the different hands of the scribes, though the variation may also have been used for showing the different vowels.

When the qualities and the places of utterance of the phonemes were definitely known, the numeral script was invented, which is self-illuminating.

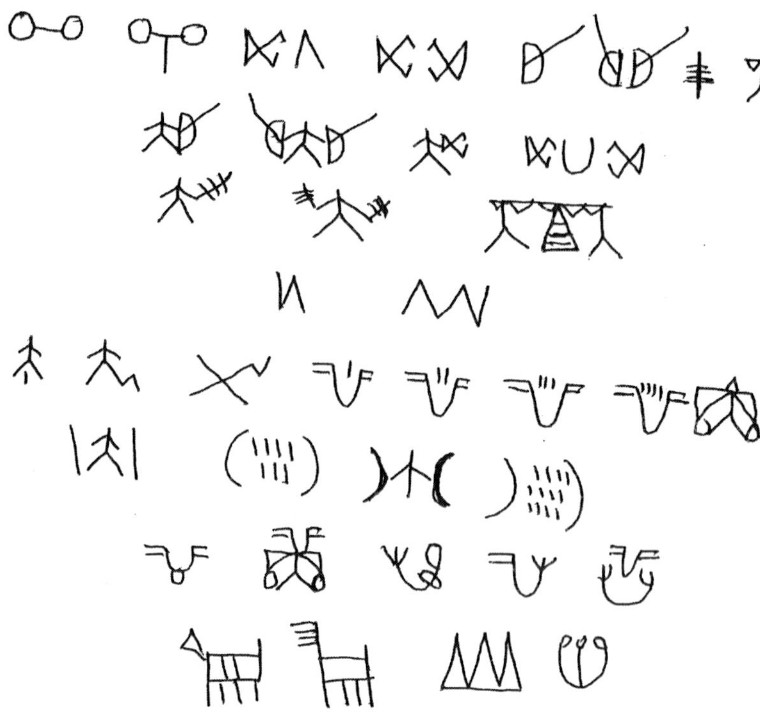

(*see* page 7) The first line of the vowels is incomplete. From the VI line, the consonants, running upwards from right to left, begin with h̲a and end with ha. This numeral order of the Indus syllabary is imaginable through the following Māheśvarasūtras, running downwards from left to right, the consonants beginning with ha and ending with h̲a:

	10	*9*	*8*	*7*	*6*	*5*	*4*	*3*	*2*	*1*
I		a	i	u	ṛ	ḷ	e	o	ai	au
II						ha	ya	va	ra	la
III						ña	ma	ṅa	ṇa	na
IV	jha	bha	gha	ḍha	dha	ja	ba	ga	ḍa	da
V	kha	pha	cha	ṭha	tha	ca	ṭa	ta	ka	pa
VI	śa	ṣa	sa	h̲a						

There are obvious disorders: The first line of the vowels does not follow the Indus order, which would have been (if running from left to right): a u i o e au ai āu āi. Pāṇini had to apologise for not beginning the vowels with u (ū3kālo'j-jhrasva-dīrgha-plutaḥ). The numerals for ma and ṅa as well as for kha and cha are not there. And the Sanskrit school has also exchanged the places of cha and kha as well as sa and ṣa to adjust the three sibilants with the voiceless stops. The placing of the voiceless stops too is arbitrary, perhaps in the original list itself, because ka and pa employ the smaller size.

The phonemes at the beginning were more frequently employed in the language than at the end, but ta ṭa were as numerous as ka pa.

Kha pha and ka pa do not have the corresponding sibilants. So the Sanskrit school put them at the two ends of the group which had them.

That is to say, we cannot be guided by the order of the Māheśvarasūtras with closed eyes in case of the numerals. The V line of the numerals reads: cha pha kha ṭha tha ca ṭa ta ka pa. The VI line reads: śa sa ṣa ẖa.

There are some examples of the numeral signs taking diacritic for a vowel: bhū vi śi ṭho ḍho (*see* below).

The Indus scribes knew how to disambiguate two numeral signs: because la and ra, written in succession, may give rise to va, they slanted the one or the other: = la ra, = ra la. Sometimes, either the one or the other is made wavy: ci va ra sa.

The little strokes ‘ “ “‘ ““ are identifiable as diacritic for u i o e, but it cannot be said whether 5 6 7 8 carry them further as au ai āu āi. As a was inherent in every consonant, it had no diacritical mark.

Some signs of the Indus texts have been identified by reading the texts, because they reflect in the worn-out and reduced vocables of the Vedic language:

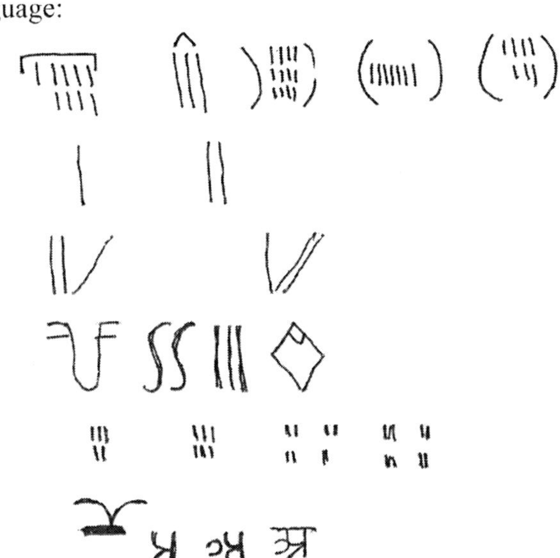

3
The Field Symbols of the Indus Texts

The Indus texts are peculiar in being very small. In defence of its propriety it may be said that the language is at the isolating stage of the ur-Sanskrit, where there is no grammar and the words are monosyllabic. Hardly more than a subject + verb or an oblique case + subject + verb are there in a clause. In this primitive form of the language anything cannot be narrated properly. One cannot write a story in this form of the language. One can describe an object but cannot name it; for example, the river Sarasvatī is just called ṣa ra ṣa (from the mountain flows and stops at the sea). But the singers of the RV knew it as 'abounding in ponds'. We do not know how much time it took in turning the clause ṣa ra ṣa into the phrase sa-ra-sa which was reduced to sáras (pond) and took the possessive suffix -vat, because it was the ponds or pools of waters in the dry seasons which highlighted the massive river in the RV.

The material culture of a community does not correspond to the growth of its language. The material culture advances by leaps and bounds and leaves the language far behind. We notice that, in the modern world, there is prosperity at its dizzy heights but the chief languages of the world are in the analytic state. Though we confuse an analytic language with isolating in definition, it must be distinctly stated that the isolating stage is the very beginning of a language, there being no grammar in it, while the analytic is the very end of this stream, which has seen all the typological stages of its development, namely isolating, agglutinative and inflexional, keeping with it a minimum but essentials of grammar.

From the excavations carried out at various sites on the Indus basin and elsewhere in the neighbourhood of this area, we form an idea of a very advanced civilisation. The people may be supposed to have reached great heights in material prosperity. But we see that the language was extremely primitive. There was almost a civil war between the linguistic backwardness and material advancement. They were marching forward in the uncultivated areas full of harmful animals and reptiles, founding new villages. Their agricultural activities had various dimensions from farming to horticulture. Their civil administration was conscious of the rogue elements of the society, which later reflect in the Dāsas and Dasyus. A vast empire was in making.

Those intelligent people of such an advanced culture must have thought out plans to make their language more expressive, at least of their own standard. First of all, they gave a visible form to their language, because an enlightened society requires a written language to control the public. As the syllables were words, which referred to birds and animals as well as to the objects of the advanced technology, they just pictographed the easiest of them and the language came in the written form. The only peculiarity would have been the fact that the pictures of the referends would have been restricted to the sounds, not to the objects and beings. That is to say, when they pictographed a turtle for ka, that sound stood for all objects and beings referred to by ka, that is, water, sun, fire, etc. When this was achieved, they expanded the ideas conveyed by small clauses. Only one syllable was an 'order', but a clause consisting of subject + verb, etc. was in the indicative mood. We do not see any definite past tense in the texts, but there is future tense and imperative mood in the later texts. The text ṇa ga (5094) simply means: the light is going away. Indirectly, it says: the darkness is coming. Then it may also suggest: it is very soon going to be the dark night. It cannot say anything more. But this clause is supplemented with the picture of a unicorn, a wild beast of very harmful nature. It may then add the following ideas: as the night will be dark, one may be attacked by some rogue elements in the society or by the animals. It may also indirectly advise that one should not go out at night, because there might be danger to life. This little picture may say so many things which can be expressed in a whole paragraph.

Another text ṣa ṭha(8013) has layers of phonetic and semantic development. As the vocabulary of the primitive communities changed from generation to generation on account of their nomadic habits, at the earliest period it simply said: the foetus rolls out of the womb of the animal (because then it related to a milch cattle delivering a calf). At the time when the upper level of the society spoke the inflexional form of the ur-Sanskrit, the same clause at the lower level of the society later meant: the egg of the universe rolled forth in the beginning. It has its shadow in the RV (10, 121, 1): hiraṇyagarbhaḥ samavartāgre. It describes some cosmogonic fact. As it is supplemented by the field symbol of a man on a kino tree looked at by a tiger from below, it seems to suggest the following idea: the calf is a soft target of some evil force. It may be devoured by some wild beast. It should be kept in some safe custody till it is capable of protecting itself.

It has been observed that the same text has different field symbols and the same field symbol has different texts. Thus ra bī ṣu va ṇa ṭha (4104) has two different field symbols:

> 1. A nude female upside down with thighs drawn apart and something issuing out, two tigers standing face to face rearing on the hindlegs.
> 2. A man armed with a weapon facing a woman with dishevelled hairs and upraised arms.
>
> —*Mahadevan*

The first symbol betrays a rustic symbolisation. It is somewhat different from what Mahadevan likes to see. It is more likely to be a female animal delivering a calf. Then it certainly belongs to an earlier epoch in the social life of the Indus people.

The second symbol, though not very usual, shows some real state of affairs and belongs to some later epoch, nearer to the stage of urbanisation. This seems to draw a vivid picture of the situation.

The first clause of the text has fossilised only as ṛbīsa in Vedic, but the second clause has fossilised in two ways: as a noun vanád and as a verb vart/vṛt. In the first case, the phrase va-na-ta was accented on the central syllable and the final t was voiced to d. In the second case, the same va-na-ta was accented on the first syllable (*vánat), then a of the second syllable was lost (*vant), and n was changed to r (vart/vṛt).

The second field symbol seems to correspond with the following meaning of the text: when the fire heats the water, in the room the vapour circulates. It portrays an alarming situation, some event getting out of control, requiring some outside help. Naturally, one may be advised to raise alarm. If this text is interpreted with a past tense (when the fire heated the water, the vapour circulated in the room), this story seems to have reached the singers of the RV (2, 4, 5).

The first part of the text fossilising as ṛbīsa is 'an abyss from which warm vapours arise', and the second part fossilising as vanád is the 'fire', which Grassmann has analysed as van-ad (wood-consumer). Because the stream of the language is the same, even a fictitious analysis appears to be logical.

As the Indus society rapidly advanced in culture, some form of central heating in the chilly winter would have been invented to warm the room. This would have become dangerously suffocating and needed outside help. Therefore, the field symbol advises the people to raise alarm.

The RV (1, 117, 3 b and elsewhere) describes the horrible experiences of the Atris in ṛbīsa, who were rescued by the Aśvins. If we are not accused of flying very high, we may assume that the Vedic priests Atris were the affluent citizens of the urbanised Indus society and the Aśvins were the men of the rapid action force of the fire brigade. Even nowadays, in the countryside of India, a borsi (an earthen cavity with fire) is kept to warm the room in a chilly winter. It may be the modern version of the Vedic ṛbīsa. We have easily explained the relevance of the second symbol and the meaning of the text, because it was contiguous with the Vedic society, even though with a considerable gap of time - the Indus society being urban and the Vedic society returning to the pastoral state.

The same is not the case with the first symbol and the meaning of the text. The field symbol compels us to give a different meaning to the same text. Also because the second clause va ṇa ṭha has fossilised as the verb vṛt 'to roll, turn round', the meaning of the whole text may change drastically.

There are several layers in the same society at the same time. The people at the uppermost level of the society may be speaking a polished language and leading a sophisticated life, while at the lower level the people may differ from them in many respects. As the typology of the same language is distributed unevenly in the society, the speech at the lower level may be backward, as even now in the countryside. For such groups of people, the field symbol was still inevitable, while the people speaking the same language on the border of the inflexional stage did not require it.

As it relates to the primitive form of the society, the meaning should relate to some ordinary event. Some domesticated animal delivering a calf may be the point of reference. As soon as the calf is delivered, it staggers and is on its feet in a few minutes. It may move away from the mother and be pounced upon by the waiting beast. The two tigers rearing on their hind-legs indicate the danger to the young one. It can be killed if left uncared for. Thus the field symbol clearly indicates that the calves of the domesticated animals must be protected from the dangerous animals. If this was the indication of the field symbol, the text may be interpreted thus: as soon as the foetus (bī) comes out (ṣu) of the womb of the animal (ra), the young calf (ṇa) begins to roll (ṭha) on the earth (va) (and goes away from the mother, only to be devoured by the wolf). The text does not say much, but the symbol is illuminating.

There is a text ci h̲a ha ṇa ṣa (4314) with the field symbol of a tiger, standing before a trough. The text may be translated thus: truly said, (it is) from the mountain (that) the river comes.

This primitive language could say nothing more. But it wanted to say much more, which should have been expressed in a whole paragraph. The tiger, a fast running and ferocious beast, suggests that the river coming from the mountain is very turbulent and may be very dangerous. The tiger cannot be domesticated like a cow, but it has to be brought under control. This could be done by strong embankments, digging canals and constructing reservoirs of waters along the bed of the river. The trough put before the tiger represents reservoirs, etc. The clause ha ṇa sa, later fossilising as harṣ 'to be happy' suggests the benefit of the controlled river for agriculture and public health. The Indus Aryans had migrated to the western countries with their knowledge of the Harappan canal engineering. The English trough from the old Eng. trog from the Germanic sources is the same as the Vedic dro- in dro-ni 'a tub, vessel'.

The text ta na va ṇa ṣa (2394) is a combination of the originally two clauses ta na ṣa and va ṇa sa. When combined, the verb of the first clause disappears. It is now a phrase in an oblique case in local sense.

The ur-Sanskrit clauses have undergone several changes in meaning while reaching the Vedic stage. The meaning was very crude at the beginning, because they had given up the nomadic life long ago and settled in villages to start agriculture. On the periphery of the Vedic stage, at least three levels had grown up in the social life. The same clause had been reduced in size at the highest level of the society and had a meaning different from that at the lowest level. At the beginning, ta na ṣa had the following meaning: from the reservoirs canals are dug out. On the periphery of the Vedic stage, the society used the same clause with the following meaning: from the womb of a woman gems come out. But through the phrase stage (the gems coming out of the womb of a woman) the same clause had been reduced to the lexeme tánas 'offspring' at the upper level of the society. A verb tan 'to expand' had been deduced from tánas, because the family expands through children. Still later, tánas was further reduced to *tans tars/tṛs 'to be thirsty', because the desire for a child is a kind of thirst. We see how the word changes its meaning as there is a change in the social framework.

Somewhere between the ur-Sanskrit and the Vedic language, the clause ta na ṣa had become the phrase tana (a river from the mountain or a canal from the reservoir), when it had to be joined with another clause va ṇa ṣa.

The clause va ṇa ṣa too originally meant: in the water the aquatic animals are there. This clause travelled a long way upto the Vedic stage and, on the periphery of the Vedic language, it was reduced to vanas (in vanaspati 'plant). A verb van was deduced, which too was further reduced to varṣ/vṛṣ.

When tana and va ṇa ṣa were combined, the field symbol of a unicorn was added to convey more ideas than could be conveyed by the small text, which simply said: in the canal from the reservoir, the acquatic animals are there. But the unicorn drawn below suggested that the canal could be dangerous through floods and there could be crocodiles in it. As a matter of fact, a whole paragraph could be written on the unicorn. Though a tiger can be friend with its human attendant, the unicorn is very ungrateful and knows no friendship.

As a matter of fact, the field symbols are an old version of the modern cartoons. If words are not enough to criticise a remarkable event, the cartoons are drawn for an animated effect in modern journals. It is an intelligent way to illuminate the idea in a modern language, which is in analytic state throughout the world. The field symbols of the Indus texts are excellent inventions of the minds of those primitive people.

We can appreciate the intelligence of those people who made their crude language symbolic. The reflections of the field symbols may be seen later in the hymns of Dīrghatamas and Vāmadeva in the RV. Even now we cannot fully understand the referend described in the following stanza:

> catvāri sṛṅgās trayo asya pādā dve śīrṣe sapta hastāso asya,
> tridhā baddho vṛṣabho roravīti maho devo martyāṃ ā viveśa.

"It has four horns, three legs, two heads and seven hands. Tied in three ways, the bull roars. The great god has encompassed the mortals".

This system of texts accompanied by the field symbols may have been imitated by the Chinese for their ideographic writing system.

4
Two-Pronged Result of an Endeavour

My involvement in the decipherment of the Indus script goes back to the early 1994. By 1996, I was able to identify the sign  with the syllable ṣa. In 1997 a text in duplicate, that is, 4147 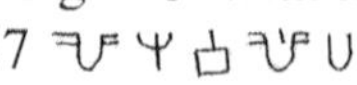 and 4132 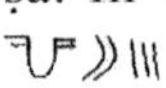 induced me to identify the meticulously arranged numerical version of the Indus script with the syllabic order of the Māheśvarasūtras of Pāṇini's grammar. With minor aberrations in the beginning, which was corrected later, it proved to be a landmark. In 1998, at least one line 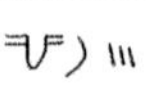 of the texts was decisively read as to its phonemic value and meaning. It was ta ṇa ṣa (read from right to left). Later its three other graphic forms were discovered, that is: 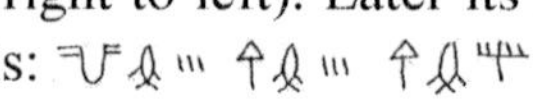

It is a clause: ta (womb) na (gem) ṣa (embryo) meaning: from the womb gems come out. Its hypothetically reduced form tánas was found to occur in the RV (5, 70, 4), meaning 'offspring', distantly agreeing with the meaning of the clause. The writing appeared to have employed three types of script, namely animal figure, geometrical figure and numeral. Although some other texts were graphically read through the mutual cooperation of the three types, and also vaguely understood, there was hardly any response from the researchers about its validity, apart from some random outright rejection.

But by 2000, I was fully convinced that the language of the Indus texts represents the isolating stage of the ur-Sanskrit and is, ultimately, the grandmother of the Vedic language.

When the relationship of the language of the Indus texts with the Vedic language was established, my attention turned from the decipherment of the Indus script to the discovery of the ancestor of Sanskrit, which is till now erroneously associated with a hypothetical parent, called Indo-European (IE).

Though initially I started with the nomenclature 'the inflexional Indus' for the IE, I found a better term 'ur-Sanskrit', which is at the isolating stage in the extant Indus texts. As the Vedic language represents a slightly later form of the inflexional stage of the ur-Sanskrit, it is not very difficult to reconstruct the intermediate agglutinative stage of the same.

The IE is a misconceived inflexional form of the ur-Sanskrit. It can be proved with some glaring examples. The reconstructed IE for 'cow' is gwōu-s, without a previous history. On the other hand, at the isolating stage of the ur-Sanskrit there was a clause gā va (goes into-the-stable: verb + oblique-case). At the agglutinative stage, it was the phrase gāva with the same body of syllables (going into the stable).When it was established as a lexeme meaning 'cow/bull' (its fem. form gāvī known to Patañjali), it was gāva-ṣa in pl. At the inflexional stage, it was reduced to gāvas due to accent on the first syllable. In Vedic it was analysed as gāv-as, the base assumed to be gāu-, in the strong forms. In weak forms the base was gau-, in the middle forms go-. But it is the story of a much later period in Vedic morphology.

When the strong form gāvas was in use, the Aryans began migrating to the western countries. In Latin, the second syllable -vas survived as bos, but the Germanic adopted the first syllable gau-, becoming cu in old English. The Latin bos entered old English through the Norman source as boef, bef, as later seen in the English beef. The English calf also seems to have developed from the acc. pl. gā-s through the Germanic source.

Similarly, what was dajha for 10 in the ur-Sanskrit is reconstructed as dekm in IE. Because there are ten syllables from da to jha in the Māheśvarasūtras, da-jha stands for ten. The second syllable was an affricate in the Vedic dialect of the ur-Sanskrit. Therefore, dajha = dadz´ha was left with daz´a, and z´ was later devoiced in Vedic, ultimately becoming daśa. In the western dialects of the ur-Sanskrit, the vowel on the first syllable was raised to e, and the second consonant was velarised, also deaspirated and devoiced: Lat. dec-, Gk. deka. In Germanic, the consonant at the first syllable was devoiced and only h was left at the second syllable. In Gothic, there is taihun, Eng. ten, Germ. Zehn

The whole IE etymological dictionary needs revision.

5
The Purpose Behind the Indus Texts

Even a little enlightened society requires that its language should be in the written form for a proper communication. But there is a criticism about the Indus texts that they are very small. This smallness of the texts may be justifiably explained by stating that the language belongs to the isolating stage, which comprises monosyllabic words (consonant + vowel) and has no grammar. There are monosyllabic clauses like ra 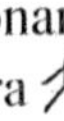, tha 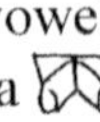, bisyllabic clauses like ṇa ga 5094, and trisyllabic clauses like ta na ṣa 1376. There are often more than one clause in the line. We can appreciate that it is the language of the most primitive community - just the beginning of a human speech. But why have such texts been written at all? There is no decisive answer to this question.

The form of the language itself may say something about it. The isolating stage of the language, of which it is the first step, portrays the most primitive type of the human society. The wandering of the tribes had now definitely stopped, which is clear from the formation of the word grāma (village): grā (wandering) + ma (end, stop). The building of houses was the next step. Their house was appropriately called dama: da (pain, suffering) + ma (end). As soon as they built houses for themselves their suffering came to an end.

When the founding of villages had made them stationary and the building of houses had made them comfortable, the chances of their meeting were considerably reduced. They were forced to invent a communication system. It was also easily achieved. Their speech consisted of monosyllabic words, each of which was the name of some animal, bird, reptile and even non-living object. They portrayed the object or being, as easily as possible, to represent the audible syllable of their speech: ka was the turtle, ga was the horns of a bull or buffalo, gha was the neck of a man, ca O was the moon, and so on. One syllable had several referends, though it was represented by the simplest form graphically. Once portrayed, ka was not only for the turtle but for all the objects, beings or ideas associated with it. And so on. Thus they developed their communication system.

In order to stop the tribe from penetrating deep into the uncultivated land, they issued the command ṣtha = stop!; in order to make them turn to left or right on the way, they wrote ṭha = turn!; advising them to go further, they indicated ra = go on! All monosyllabic clauses may be some sort of command. But the bisyllabic and longer clauses were in the indicative mood. They engraved these messages on clay-tablets, bone-rods, etc. and sent them to different villages. Writing such texts would have turned into some cottage industries. It was the ancient version of the modern post cards. That is why, there are numerous copies of the same texts.

Some of these ancient expressions are even now heard in the countryside: na is spoken to stop an animal, and so on. na is an old syllable for no. So also mā, after verbs. For yes, it was ta, as even now in the countryside.

They had moved considerably from the physical objects to the abstract ideas. Their ṇa for 'gem' was now the verbal idea 'to shine'; the same for 'water' was now for 'to flow'; nada was a river flowing with indistinct noise, and its feminine form nadī was a big river.

They conceived gha for 'future', ga for 'order', ā for the past tense, and so on. When they indicated 'future' by gha added to a verb, it was often followed by ga for 'order': dra gha, ra ga (catastrophic fire-future, speed-order = There will be a fire-tragedy, run away), pra gha, va ga (storm-future, dwelling-order = There will be a storm, take shelter in a house), etc.

When they were in need of joining two clauses through some conjunction, they simply, turned the vowel of the first clause into i or u, keeping the second to a: 4147 ga ṣu va ṇa ṣa (plants grow, because the water gives life). These were general instructions for the farming system.

Thus we see that there were very good purposes in the minds of the authors of the Indus texts. They are not the playful drawings of the illiterate people of the Indus civilisation, as unwisely and wrongly conceived by someone and announced provocatively. These texts are the ancient version of the modern journalism. They spread knowledge through the crude form of their language. Because the material culture advances more rapidly than the language, they had achieved much material success at the isolating stage of the language. The advancement of culture had, of course, obliged them to go beyond the capacity of the language. That is why, the language of the text itself is seen transiting into the agglutinative stage by the emergence of the suffix elements.

They had tried to popularise various ideas (The early Indus civilisation, 2006) on farming (pp. 14-37), weather forecast (37-38), discovery of fire (39-42), weapons for hunting (43-44), danger from reptiles and safety therefrom (45-48), domestication of animals (49-64), arts and crafts (65-91), metaphysical thoughts (92 ff), and so on.

6
Linguistic Archaeology

The texts of the Indus inscriptions have been made available to us through excavations. The archaeologists have done their job of determining the direction of writing. It is generally from right to left. This has been the greatest contribution of the archaeology, because the reading of the text in the usual left to right direction was making the decipherment ab initio invalid.

A real progress in reading has been possible through a meticulous comparison of the syllable order of Māheśvarasūtras with the scrupulously arranged numeral signs of the Indus script. The numeral signs have helped further in the syllabic identification of the animal and geometrical signs. Thus a large portion of the texts is readable syllabically.

The Indus texts thus read partly reflect, more or less, in the sharply reduced and decomposed body of the conspicuously oldest words of the language of the RV, as seen through the naked eyes.

The text 1555 reads ṇa ṇa ṣu ni śa da bha ṣa, which is doubtless.

Graphically, the first clause terminates at the third syllable; ṇa ṇa ṣu. Because the verb is bent towards u, it may be supposed to be syntactically related with the rest of the text.

The second part of the text seems to have two clauses with a common verb ṣa at the end. Thus the two clauses may be distinctly shown: ni śa ṣa and da bha ṣa.

The last clause da bha ṣa may have contracted as "dabhas in Vedic, but later devoiced and deaspirated as tapas 'penance'. Of course, there are verbs deduced from both, namely dabh 'to injure' and tap 'to be hot', having divergent meanings.

The preceding clause ni śa (ṣa) may have contracted as niś 'night', but this meaning is secondary, developing from some earlier primary meaning. An x-ray examination of niś 'night' and tapas 'penance' on semantic level suggests that both these words are supposed to oppose each other. Because 'penance' is another name for 'hard work', the meaning 'night' for niś seems to have evolved from an earlier meaning 'slumber' (opposing 'hard work' in sense). Therefore, 'slumber' and 'hard work' appear to lurk in the Indus clauses ni śa ṣa and da bba ṣa. Now we should come to their interpretation.

The clause ni śa ṣa should mean: inactivity causes slumber. On the other hand, da bha ṣa should mean: pain causes activity. There may be other meanings too around the periphery of the two clauses. But this is the basis of the development of the meanings 'night' for niś and 'penance' for tapas.

Before transiting into tapas, the earlier vocable dabhas must have meant 'hard work, which was the first ladder for the descent of meaning.

'Slumber' and 'hard work' must be the object of the introductory clause ṇa ṇa ṣu, which has to be interpreted in this light. Because this clause has already an object in front of it, this clause consists of subject + 2 verbs. The subject ṇa, represented through the animal sign, means 'a man'. The following verb ṇa means 'know' and ṣa means 'see'. The whole text now means: A man must know and see: inactivity causes slumber (and) pain causes activity.

This text exhorts people to postpone slumber for the night and engage in hard work. They had given up the nomadic life. The villages had been founded and houses were built. Lest they become lazy, they were asked to be hard working. The study of the Indus texts is really a linguistic archaeology.

7
Winding of Straws

In the Indian countryside, we often find the villagers passing the hot hours of the day under the shade of a tree, winding the bunch of straws to make a rope. It is reminiscent of an old tradition, of a form of the cottage industry, in those days.

A part of some Indus texts given below reads śa ṭha:

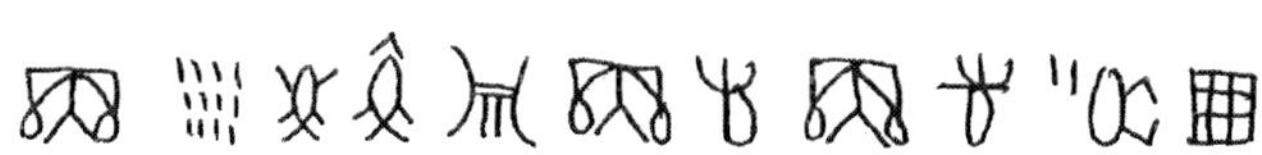

Though the whole text is not comprehensible, also not readable śa ṭha seems to have transited into something as explained below:

The syllable ṭha (disc, circle) as a verb means 'to turn round, to wind'. The preceding syllable śa[1] may have been for 'a bunch of straw', which was perhaps ten in number – halved equally in course of winding. The winding agents too were ten – the five fingers of the two hands. Then śa ṭha seems to say: ten fingers turn round a bunch of ten straws. It might also be in the form of order. As the product of 'winding', śa ṭha suffered phonetically and also semantically to become saṭa, saṭā 'the mated hairs of an ascetic', but its another phonetic development was śata (ten times ten), meaning 100. Before this word came out, the Aryans had left the original homeland, because the word, is recorded with various plus elements in other languages (Lat. Centum, Gk. hekaton).

1 śa is the initial syllable in śara 'reed'. Even śara 'an arrow' is so called because it was originally made of the hard stem of the reed.
Vocabulary: śa = ten ṭha = to wind

8
Sheep Breeding

u la h̲a pa ja 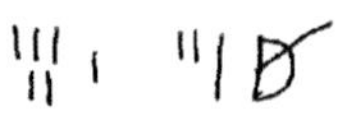

The reading of the above text is reliable. But in its original form, as a clause of the isolating stage of the ur-Sanskrit, it hardly gives any sense. However, it is true that there are two clauses here: u la h̲a and pa ja.

The first clause u la h̲a has suffered two important changes before it is urā 'sheep' at the inflexional Vedic stage: the second syllable has undergone rhotacism and the third syllable has lost the fricative h̲. Thus it is u ra a = urā. When urā 'sheep' is the fossilised form of the clause, the meaning may be attempted with the background of a sheep.

Because va means 'dwelling', u also may be supposed to mean something like 'enclosure' in the oblique case, and then la should mean 'sheep', necessarily the subject. And h̲a is the verb, probably meaning 'to run away'. The whole clause perhaps says: From the enclosure the sheep run away. A wolf is said to be urā-mathi 'who takes away the sheep'. If the sheep is tied in the enclosure, it cannot get out and be taken away by the wolf.

Therefore, pa ja may be supposed to mean: tie up the animal. Naturally, pa is for 'animal', reflecting in the Vedic paśu (animal). The affricate ja has split as dźa, and then ź has been devoiced as ś. With its nominal value, pa śa has turned into paśu (the tied up). We know how the ur-Sanakrit da-jha (= da dźha) has become daśa in Vedic through the same process.

The whole text seems to say: from the enclosure the sheep run away (and are killed by the wolves); tie up the animals (in the enclosure).

We see how the pastoral primitive society says something which only resounds in the later culture. The Indus texts are to be interpreted as much linguistically as archaeologically. The dust of phonology has covered the whole material. The meaning only sparkles through the dust.

The word paśu, dialectically pronounced pahu, transited into Latin as pecus, in Germanic as fehu (German Vieh), etc. k is the plosive version of the fricative h, which is phonemically the same as ś. We know that k, ś and h alternate in cognate languages.

Vocabulary

u = enclosure, la = sheep, ha = to run away, pa = animal, ja = to tie up.

9
A Water-Channel for Irrigation

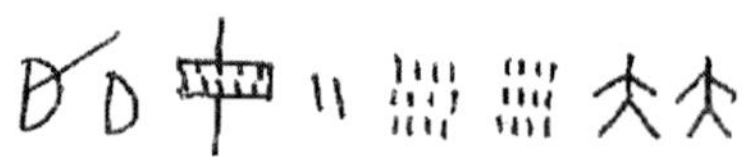

This text reads as follows: ra ra śa śa ẖa tta va u. The only sign which is doubtful in reading is the 6th from the right. Singly it is ta; but when one is put on the other upside down, it is probably tta. If the identification of this sign is correct, it is a pleasant breakthrough. In spite of even the correct reading, it is very difficult to understand the text, because there is no help from Sanskrit.

A clue to understanding comes from a rustic word of some village dialect. This word is hattā (as pronounced nowadays). It is a small channel or a simple cavity with two walls from two sides to let the water flow. The construction of this channel itself gives some clue to the understanding of the text.

Though the walls are two, each on right and left side of the channel, ra (the wall on the one side) and śa (the wall on the other side) are written twice, as if to emphasise the width of the walls. A broad wall must be there from two sides, not to let the waters escape. Being at the beginning, they are in oblique case, expressing the idea of 'between'. The next phrase ẖa tta is in instrumental. Now the whole text may be interpreted thus: Between the two walls, through the channel or cavity, the waters flow.

It is a primitive version of the canal engineering, which is practised even now in the remote countryside. The waters were carried through this channel from some distant reservoirs or river to irrigate the agricultural lands. The instrument to siphon water from the reservoirs is called ḍhos nowadays.

It is wonderful that even the words of the early ur-Sanskrit is preserved today in the rustic speech of the countryside.

As this message was to be carried to different villages and districts under the civil administration, several copies of it were made for wide circulation.

In another text, 2431 tta is at the beginning from the right in the first line. Though the text is not properly readable, it may be supposed that this text runs from left to right, so that tta comes at the end and becomes pronounceable.

10
The Fertilising Waters

Bhū ma na 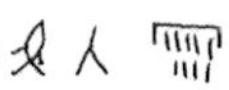
(On the earth the milk flows)

The reading of the text is doubtless. The first sign is definitely bha due to its numeral order in the ur-Māheśvarasūtra, and the diacritic over it is hardly anything but for ū. The second sign is most certainly ma, as verified from other readings. The third sign is undoubtedly for na. This Indus clause bhū ma na has fossilised in Vedic as the little used vocable bhūman, meaning primarily 'earth' and secondarily 'abundance' due to its association with the earth, accompanied by shift of accent on the last syllable: bhumán. The primary meaning 'earth' is really the clue to the interpretation of this clause, because the subject of the clause is generally retained in meaning even when it is fossilised as a vocable. The first syllable bhū itself is 'earth', as attested through bhū, bhū-mi 'earth', etc. Though ma means both 'water' and 'milk', the latter is intended here only to glorify 'water' for an agrarian primitive society. The water, being the gift of the nature, is not less than milk for the earth. Thus the clause bhū ma na means: On the earth the milk flows. This refers to a situation when it has rained abundantly after a scorching summer.

A joyful reflection of this situation may be found in the Parjanya-sūkta of the RV (e.g. 5,83,8). The Vedic singer compares the water with the clarified butter: Draw up the great bucket, pour it down; let the stream released flow forward. Drench heaven and earth with ghee; let there be a good drinking place for the cows.

Vocabulary

bhū = earth ma = milk, water na = to flow.

11
In a Dental Clinic

As each syllable of the ur-Sanskrit was independently a monosyllabic word, śa da bha ṣa is a text quite independent of ṇa ṇa ṣu ni śa da bha ṣa, the initial śa of the smaller text breaking away from the preceding ni of the longer text, which formed a clause ni śa together there.

In the smaller text, there are two bisyllabic clauses: śa da and bha ṣa. They have fossilised as two Vedic verbs:

	śa da		bha ṣa
	śad		bhas
(1)	to fall out	(1)	to chew
(2)	to excel	(2)	to push

We see that the phonetic development of the Indus clauses into the Vedic roots is crystal clear. But how the meaning of each clause has squeezed into a single verbal idea can be ascertained only if the meanings of the individual syllables are known.

Incidentally, the passage dantās te śatsyanti AV 11, 3, 37 (Your teeth will fall down) seems to be a paraphrasing of the Indus clause śa da, where śa may stand for 'fall down' and da for 'teeth'. The phoneme /ś/ is the initial sound is śak (can), śaci (power), śat (kill), śad (fall down), śapha (hoof), śap (abuse), śara (arrow), śas (kill), etc., generally having an injurious sense. The phoneme /d/ is the initial sound in dat (tooth), dad (give), dabh (injure), dam (control), dar (tear), daś (bite), dah (burn), etc., da itself meaning heat, pain, mountain, etc. in the traditional lexicon of the monosyllabic words. Both daś and śad have injurious sense.

Even bhas (chew, crush) is connected with 'teeth' in tigmā agne tava tviṣaḥ, dadbhir vanāni bapsati RV 8,43,3 (Your sharp flames chew woods with teeth). Perhaps bha = food, ṣa = consume, swallow. The phoneme bh is the initial sound in bhaj (divide, cook), bhad (good), bhid (pierce), bhū (be), bhar (bear), bhas (eat), etc. Its connection with light is remarkable later. The phoneme /ṣ/ has a dozen of meanings in the traditional lexicons, but its initial position is limited in Sanskrit, all roots beginning with ṣ in Dhp said to be regarded as those beginning with s. It can be assigned any meaning suiting the context.

The text śa da bha ṣa crudely says: decayed teeth, swallow food. In other words: if the teeth are decayed, just swallow the food.

We may have no words to explain the relevance of the text. Perhaps it forms a part of inscriptions of some hospital involving dental health. In the old age, when teeth are decayed, a man cannot chew the food. Such persons are advised to swallow the soft food.

Then we come to the point of saying that though the isolating stage of a language is incapable of expressing profound ideas, the necessities of the urban life of the society force the speakers to go beyond the capacity of the language.

Vocabulary

śa = ten da = teeth bha = food ṣa = consume

12
Dadhikrā 'The Divine Horse'

bha dha dhī gra ṣa

We may not have any doubt about the reading of the text. The central three signs dha dhī gra seem to have fossilised as dadhikrā in the RV, and it refers to the 'rolling ball of the rising sun' in the morning. Just on the basis of the meaning of this fossilised vocable dadhikrā, we may suggest that bha means 'horizon', the part of the earth which seems to meet the sky at the time of the rising of the sun. Then the apparent meaning of the clause seems to be this: From the horizon (bha) the brightly (dha) shining (dhī) sun (gra) emerges (ṣa).

The meaning of the clause cannot satisfy us unless the relevance of the text is brought to light. Many such texts have left us dumb as to what these meanings had to do with those primitive people. We are liable to question the mental horizon of the primitive people when they say something which is too high in our calculation. We are prone to underrate the high achievement of the ancient people, because our view about them is low.

When the western scholars began to study the RV, they took it to be the thoughts of a cowherd. They wrote excellent Vedic grammars, prepared exhaustive etymological dictionaries, but their views about those thoughts did not change. What Max Müller said about the hymns of the RV does not change substantially as we read Geldner's translation. Sri Aurobindo had warned against such views of the western scholars.

When the Indus texts have come before us and even when we claim to have partly read them, we are unable to convince a sceptic about their intended meanings. Once, when I told an Indian scholar that I had found the seed of the Sāvitrī-stanza in a clause of the Indus texts, his laughter was more deafening than the thunder of the rain-cloud. We have to realise that the Indus people were primitive in the sense that they spoke the ur-Sanskrit at its isolating stage. But materially and mentally they had advanced too far. The language did not go along their rapid material advance. That is why, they did not hesitate in exploiting the language beyond its capacity. They were becoming poetic even at the isolating stage of the language. Because they were living with nature, they derived inspiration from them. The ball of the rising sun rolling towards them inspired their intellect, excited them to activity. The Savitṛ-sūktas of the RV are inspired by such little Indus clauses.

The scorching rays of the hot sun (ta gra ṣa ra) of an Indus text had become the 'inspiring light of the divine sun' (savitur vareṇyaṃ bhargo devasya) in the RV (3,61,10). We also know, how the cooking fire of the early generations was not the same when the thinkers of the Upaniṣads said: agne naya supathā... This jump of ideas compels us to think as to how they looked at the different objects of the nature. The powers of the objects of nature were personified in the form of gods, which we do not generally realise.

This digression was necessary to point out the relevance of the Indus texts. In the RV, the fossilised dadhikrā has the meaning which is not widely apart from the meaning of the Indus clause. But the imposition of the idea of a 'divine horse' is the result of wonderful imagination on the part of this singer of the RV. The idea of the divine horse arose out of the speed of the rolling ball of the morning sun. It is the step preceding the conception of dadhy-añc (later dadhīca, dadhīci) which, however, relates to a human being. As long as the ball of the morning sun appeared to be rolling, it was dadhikrā (conceived to be a divine horse), but as the ball was enveloped in the strong sun-light and appeared to move in the bow-shape through the sky, it was dadhyañc (the glorious bending). In the afternoon, there was a heavy rainfall, because Vṛtra was supposed to have been killed through the bow by Indra. The myths are made by joining the broken knots of events in the nature. There is continuity in the myths of dadhikrā, dadhyañc and Indra. Just after dadhikrā, somewhere on the course of dadhyañc, there lies the knot of Savitṛ 'coming through the dark space and seeing all creatures, driving away hardships (RV 1, 35, 2-3). Of course, the dadhikrā aspect of the sun could not endure the competing subsequent aspects of the sun. The bow made out of the backbone of Dadhīci killed Vṛtra. The sunny day gave ample waters to the thirsty fields in the mid-summer.

The agrarian society of the Indus people is the background of the Vedic culture, though the gap between them is dusky. Briefly, dadhikrā is the personified powerful speed of the ball of the rising sun in the morning, exhorting the people for the routinely daily work.

The Indus sign for dha  looks like the spinal cord of a human being sitting on hunch, representing the bow-shaped movement of the sun in the sky, which may be responsible for the dadhīca-myth in Puranic age.

The gra syllable of the Indus texts reflects through gl - at the beginning of words (e.g. Eng. glamour, German Glut, etc.) with the inherent sense of 'light' in the Germanic languages. It is cl- in Latin (clarus, etc.) and -kra in Vedic dadhikrā.

Vocabulary

bha = horizon dha = brilliant (ly) dhī = shining
gra = sun ṣa = to emerge

13
The Old Age

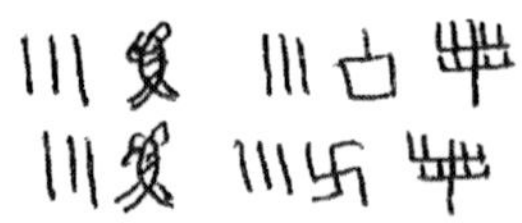

The text la va va śa va has a partially duplicate version, where va  is represented by the Svastika sign . Though there is no doubt about the reading, what the text intends to say is not easily clear.

The text has apparently two clauses la va va and śa va. The final va in each clause seems to be the verb. One of the meanings of va in the traditional lexicon of the monosyllabic words is an 'arrow'. This may suggest its having the meaning 'to harm, injure, kill'.

Then the syllable preceding the verb is va in the first clause and śa in the second. They are naturally the objects, but their meanings have to be found out.

The first syllable la of the text seems to be the subject of both the clauses. It means perhaps 'time'. The two clauses may be separately put thus: la va va + la śa va.

If va, the verb, means 'to kill' and la, the subject, means 'time', the object must be some 'soft target'. The time makes one old. The oldness is a harm caused by time to something. The first object expressed by va is perhaps 'strength' (the meaning given to va in the traditional lexicon). The second object expressed by śa is 'body' (śa being the first syllable of śarīra, which is derived from the Vedic root śṛ 'to perish'). The text seems to say: the time kills strength, the time kills the body. Here we may make some emendation in the name of the subject. It is (not 'time' but) the 'old age'. The text means to say: the old age kills strength (and) kills the body.

The second clause has naturally contracted as śava 'dead body' (which is artificially derived from the Vedic root śu/śva/śvi 'to swell'). The first clause la va va is not readily recognisable in some fossilised form, unless rūpa 'form, appearance' is its decomposed body (which is said to be cognate with varpas). But the word rūpa from lūva from la-u-va from la va va is not impossible.

If our interpretation is even distantly correct, we can suppose that the people were progressing very rapidly in thought. They were forced to exploit the language even beyond its capacity. The isolating stage of the language is not capable of carrying such messages.

Vocabulary

la = old age, va = 1. strength 2. to kill, śa = body.

14

The Pre-Vedic vanád 'fire' and rám 'ash'

In the Vedic philology, a word is traced to its immediate root. Otherwise, it is said to be 'of unknown origin', which is the only honest way to explain it.

Many stanzas of the RV, while addressing or celebrating a deity, Agni for example, are incomprehenslble not only through their obscure words but also through a scrappy reference to some pre-historic event. These stanzas could stand by themselves as little ballads, but they were reluctantly included in a hymn addressed to the relevant deity. Their abrupt inclusion is just tolerated.

The following stanza relates to Agni:

> ā yán me ábhvaṃ vanádaḥ pánanta, uśígbhyo nā́mimīta várnam,
> sá citréṇa cikite rā́ṃsu bhāsā́, jujurvā́ṃ yó múhur ā́ yúvābhū́t. 2, 4, 5.

In the first hemistich, there is some correspondence in the case-forms of the two verses (a:b):

a	*b*	
abhvam	varṇam	object
ā pananta	amimīta	verb
vanadaḥ	-	possessive
me	uśigbhyaḥ	indirect object

If mi/mā (śabde) in b. means 'to inform, communicate, convey', varṇa may be the 'information, news', and uśij may be the 'one to whom the news is communicated, the public in general'. Correspondingly, in a. the indirect object (me = to me) is possibly the Vedic singer himself. The verb ā-pan is not very different from mi/mā in meaning. The word vanád was obscure and uncertain before Grassmann analysed it as van (wood) - ad (consumer), meaning 'fire'. Even abhva has become a little more comprehensible after Geldner has conceived it as 'the smoky form of the fire before it is in flames'. And abhva of vanád is the object of the verb ā-pan.

We easily ignore the importance of the past form and render it by present. Why did the poet then use the past form? The imperfect in the first verse is followed by the pluperfect in the second, as if the narration of some past event is the point of reference. The situation relates to some event in the pre-historic period.

There is an Indus text which reads thus: ra bī ṣu va ṇa ṭha (no. 4304: Mahadevan). It means: when the fire (ra) heated (ṣu) the water (bī), in the dwelling (va) the vapour (ṇa) circulated (ṭha). As the language is very primitive, it cannot by itself express the accompanying ideas. Therefore, it has been supplemented by the field symbol of 'a woman with dishevelled hairs and upraised arms, a man standing before her with some rescue material'. It is a sort of cartoon to give a suggestive account of the incident. Perhaps there was a tragic conflagration, and the victims were rescued after great damage to the property.

The first clause of the Indus text has fossilised as ṛbīsa (a cavity in the earth from which hot vapours arise). It is impossible to derive it from some Vedic root. The second clause has fossilised as van-ad, ingeniously analysed by Grassmann as van-ad (wood-consumer). The singers of the RV as well as the compilers of the Saṃhitā text knew vanád as 'fire'. Because the stream of the Indus and Vedic language is the same, even a fictitious analysis becomes logical and reasonable.

The clause va ṇa ṭha has otherwise also fossilised as vart (vṛt) 'to roll', suggesting other meaning of the same clause, the text accompanied by another field symbol on the other side. The two-way fossilisation of va ṇa ṭha may be shown in the following way:

1. va ṇa ṭha > vanata > vanád (the final t voiced due to the preceding accent).
2. va ṇa ṭha > vanata > vant > vart (vṛt), the central ṇa losing a and undergoing rhotacism, [when accented on the first syllable].

While interpreting this stanza, we are tempted to go back to a prehistoric period in the urbanised Indus society, when there was a central heating system for the dwellings in the chilly winter. The RV 1,116,8. 117,3. 5,78,4. 10,39,9 describe the horrible experiences of the Atris in ṛbīsa and their rescue by the twin-gods Aśvins. Here we imagine that the

Atris were the affluent citizens of the urbanised Indus society and the Aśvins formed a two-man team of the rapid action force of the fire-brigade. The Aśvins used to rush at once to control the situation. The word aśvin is derived from the same root as the adj. āsu (fast, quick, also adv. soon, at once). The Aśvins were neither the horse-men nor some aspect of the nature. They were the officials of the pre-historic civil administration. Even ṛbīsa would originally have been some luxurious dwelling chamber, fitted with central heating system.

After the collapse of the urban Indus culture, there was the beginning of the pastoral Vedic culture. The affluent Atris trapped in fire were now the fire-priests, one of them later being a house-holder sage with his wife Anasūyā, and the Aśvins were the twin-gods of controversial description, later being the divine physicians, called Aśvinī-kumāras. The Indus history is the basis of the Vedic mythology The interval between the Indus and Vedic cultures was as much as the time taken by the clauses fossilising as words. Now we are in a position to attempt interpretation of the stanza.

The word vanád is specifically the smoky and suffocating fire of ṛbīsa. It is different from the fire of the kitchen or of the sacrificial altar. In another version of ṛbīsa, some specific fruits are matured through steaming from outside. The modern version of ṛbīsa is borsī, which is used to warm the room in the chilly winter in the countryside. The word abhva may be 'the dangerous situation' caused by the suffocating fire of ṛbīsa.

This singer of the RV wants to say that the fire tragedy in the pre-historic Indus society was terrible and devastating. But, as the public memory is proverbially very short, much was gradually forgotten till it reached the Vedic singer. By that time, it was just a simple incident.

Now we can come to the second hemistich. Here saḥ in the verse c. certainly refers to vanád of a. The word rám 'ash' is the fossilised form of the Indus phrase rama (the extinguished fire). Though it has been properly highlighted by the editor of the pada-text, Roth failed to enter it in his dictionary. The second hemistich intends to state the cause of the tragedy, but puts it just as a fact. Perhaps a little particle of fire was the cause of the tragedy. It was lurking in the ashes and was going to be extinguished. But it was inflamed through some external cause. Soon it engulfed the whole house, as if an old man became young again.

A straightforward translation of the stanza is as follows:

> The horror of the fire which was reported to me (the singer) was known to the public as a simple incident. That (fire) was lurking

> in the ashes with sparkling lustre which, (though) grown old, became young again.

After we have interpreted the stanza as transparently as possible, the question arises: was it necessary to include an irrelevant event of the bygone age abruptly in a hymn to Agni?

The story of the fire-tragedy was faintly alive in the public memory, and this stanza of the RV would have been current in the form of a little ballad. Because the compilers of the Saṃhitā text knew the tragic fire by the name of vanád, this stanza was included in this hymn to Agni. The Vedic singer would have been a little surprised to note that Agni, which could be so ferocious, is adored in the society. He appears to look at the fire of the kitchen on the one hand and at the fire-god of the social rituals on the other.

But we should realise that the crude Agni of the early civilisation was not exactly the same by the time of the RV. Semantically, it had undergone several transformations before it reached the singers of the RV. Agni of the RV is more abstract than concrete, more metaphorical than literal.

While the cooking fire was burning in the kitchen of the Indus society, the ur-Sanskrit was stagnating at the isolating stage with the monosyllable words and little grammar. Then Agni was the clause 'a gni' meaning 'it produces light'. When the material life of the people had advanced and touched great heights, the primitiveness of the language was matched by introducing field symbols along with the texts to express the horror of the fire. When rituals were introduced in the social life of the people and the language transited to the agglutinative stage, the fire of the kitchen had shifted to the sacrificial altar. This fire began to be identified with knowledge, because both of them converge on brightness. The knowledge is the brightness residing in the human mind. The brightness was later identified with truth, and the fire itself was ultimately conceived as truth. The language too came to the inflexional stage. The society, language and thought were progressing simultaneously in parallel. They reached a climax.

Later, the truth itself, the abstract representation of the fire, was again conceived anthropomorphically, described in ritual terms, namely: butter-backed, flame-haired, tawny-bearded, sharp-jawed and golden-toothed. These traits were super-imposed on the truthful and enlightened human beings of the society. That is to say, the bearded wise and truthful men of the society in that prehistoric age were called Agni by the singers of the RV.

We have no idea of the period when this culture collapsed. But its existence reflects in Vedic through the fossilised words and the scrappily narrated stories in the Vedic hymns.

The Vedic singer had the memory of such enlightened human beings of the bygone age, who were identified with or simply called Agni. In the Vedic mythology, they came to be classed with gods, who were in close communion with the ordinary human beings of the society. When they spoke, they appeared to bellow like a bull, shone like sun, and were at the head of everything, the so-called Purohitas. Therefore, in the RV 1,189 Agni is implored to lead through right path, and so on. The Upanisads sing the glory of such divine Agnis.

The ordinary fire of the kitchen had reached this height of the human thoughts, when the singers of the RV were celebrating Agni. The truth is as bright as the fire. But just as the fire is concealed in ashes, the bright truth is often covered with dusky falsehood. When Gṛtsamada says that the fire was lurking in the ashes, he also means to say that truth is often concealed in or besmeared with falsehood.

That is why, Swami Dayanand insists that the Vedic mantras are to be interpreted on material as well as spiritual levels. Sri Aurobindo also has endorsed this view.

The word vanád occurs only once in the RV, but rám 'ash' occurs in the RV 4,1,8 once more:

> sá dūtó víśvéd abhí vaṣṭi sádmā, hótā híraṇyaratho ráṃsu-jihvaḥ,
> rohíd-aśvo vapuṣyó vibhāvā, sádā raṇvah pitumatī́va saṣat.

Here ram forms a Bahuvóhi compound raṃsu-jihva, retaining its loc. pl. form as the first member. The pada-text separates the two members as ráṃ + ṣu-jihva, as if it wants to highlight the first member ram. The compound intends to give the meaning 'having the tongue (concealed) in ashes', rather than 'pleasant-tongued' as suggested by others.

If the intention of the editors of the pada-text has been properly understood, raṃsu-jihva seems physically to refer to 'a fiery log of wood with its tip besmeared with ashes'. This may be the literal or surface meaning. Its deeper meaning is much profound.

If we consider Agni to be just the fire of the kitchen or of the sacrificial altar, we cannot really go any further and are bound to miss the target, because we are at the two ends of two homogenous cultures. As a matter of fact, Agni is that human personage of the bygone age, now raised to divinity, who, in his capacity as a wise and truthful official or public man of the society used to visit all social gatherings as a messenger of the civil administration. He provoked people to do their duties. He used to move on a golden car drawn by tawny horses, himself having excellent body, shining form and smiling face. His 'tongue concealed in ashes' is metaphorical and suggests that he spoke sarcastically without offending others. He was the guardian of truth. Agni was, thus, not the cooking fire of the kitchen or even of the sacrificial altar to the singers of the RV. It was the human personage, raised to divinity, who was called Agni by the people. Agni was, that is to say, an office or position.

Translation

He is a messenger, visits all assemblies, is exhorter, has a golden car, has a sarcastic tongue, has tawny horses and beautiful form, is resplendent and has a smiling face. He is like a feast hall abounding in good food.

15
A Canal

A Canal from the Main River

This text may be assumed to be in the typical Gāyatrī metre. There are nine syllables for nine ideas, each clause, which is a pāda, consists of three syllables. The following reading too may be reliable as best as possible: ni nda ṣo ni ha nu va ṇa ṣa.

The first two clauses have their verbs turned towards o and u respectively, showing that they are related with the last clause syntactically.

In a different text, the first clause has been interpreted thus: On the wall (ni) a hole (nda) there is (ṣa). This meaning is just symbolic. Any meaning can be deduced from it, depending on context. To account for the relevance of the last clause, the meaning of which, though itself stated symbolically, is almost well-known (from the water life comes = plants grow through waters), the first clause may be said to mean the following: From the (main) river (ni) a canal (nda = hole) is dug (ṣo). The second clause then gives a relevant meaning: through the (dug out) canal vegetations (ha) grow on (nu). It is not necessary to justify the assumed meaning of a syllable in every case. The meanings of a syllable given in the traditional lexicon are just symbolic, knowingly expressed vaguely, so that any suitable meaning can be supposed.

The fossilised forms of the clauses ni nda ṣo and ni ha nu have semantically become obscure, though the same of va ṇa ṣa, namely vanas, is still comprehensible.

The interpretation of the text is based on common sense. The language at the isolating stage is a mindless creature, just breathing in and breathing out, and moving instinctively. In its living state, the language was fully comprehensible to the speakers and listeners, because the context was clear to them. In its written form, that context has gone out of sight. Only its fossil in the later stage of the language can suggest what it could have meant earlier.

The last clause of the text is the clue, which is fortunately clear, more or less. The horticulture is the subject matter. The means of this project are shown in the first two clauses, step by step: first the canal, then the distribution of waters. The third is the result. Let a canal be there from the main river. The vegetations will grow. In life there will be happiness.

Vocabulary

ni = a big and long river, then also a canal
nda = hole, gap > canal
ṣa = come out, dig out
ha = breath: vegetation, plant
na > nu = continuity, grow
va = water
ṇa = life.

16

The Sky is Qualified by the Sound

śabdaika-guṇa ākāsaḥ
ni ha ṣa-ṭha la-ra

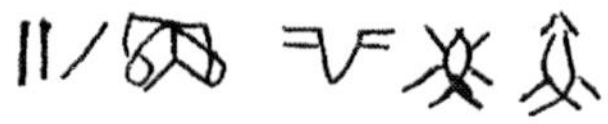

The reading of this text is assumed to be reliable. The numeral sign for la is slanted towards right to avoid the making of va by its combination with the sign for ra.

The first four syllables appear to make a clause, ṣa-ṭha being the verb ṣa (be) in the past tense (= was, there was). Then the preceding ha is its subject and ni preceding the latter is in oblique case. The meaning of the clause ni ha ṣa-ṭha (oblique case + s + v) has to be ascertained.

Phonetically, ni ha seems to have fossilised as nih f.

AV 2, 6, 5:	áti ního áti sṛ́dhó	'tyácittīr áti dviṣaḥ
VS 27, 6:		'tyácittim átyárātim agne

In the company of the action nouns sṛdh (enmity), acitti (ignorance), dviṣ (envy), nih may be an action noun. Therefore, Mahīdhara's ni-hantṛ (killer), an agent noun, is not acceptable. It is just a guess on the basis of the final h. Even Roth's proposal to read nido for niho cannot be accepted, when nih is no more a ghost-word. But nih is semantically identical with nid f. (= nindā 'censure'), because ha in āha (said) is identical with da in vada (speak in human voice), gada (sound distinctly) nada (sound indistinctly) in meaning. That is to say, ha means sound, voice, speech. If it is so, ni is 'sky' which is said to be full of sound. Now, the meaning of the clause ni ha ṣa-ṭha seems to emerge: In the sky (ni) the sound (ha) there was (ṣa-ṭha). The past tense appears to express the eternal truth.

The last syllables, la (mind, intellect, understanding) ra (fire), perhaps say: learn : know : Cf. Old Eng. Lar, Eng. Lore, learn.

The whole text appears to say: The sky is full of sound, Know or learn this truth. It was later scientifically formulated in the Sāṅkhya philosophy : śabdaika-guṇa ākāśaḥ (The chief quality of the ether is the sound).

This text has been very interesting. Its ni ha has authenticated a Vedic vocable. Even the presence of la-ra in the Germanic languages is not less wonderful. The d sound in Latin dire is not different from the same in Vedic vad, etc.

Mahadevan has listed ||/ and |// as single conjunct signs. We see that they are the bisyllabic la ra and ra la respectively. At least la-ra is a bisyllabic verb meaning 'to learn'. Even ra ls may be seen in Eng. rale from Fr. raler 'to rattle'. ra la, when it was a clause, would have meant: the fire rattles. Both la and ra have slanting to avoid their coming together as va-syllable.

The phonetic connection of the cognate words in related languages is easily established, but the semantic connection is correspondingly very difficult. When there is a little phonetic change in a word, the meaning jumps like a frog in unpredictable direction. We cannot easily understand how the positive statement (there is sound in the sky) appeared negatively (censure, scorn) in Vedic. It seems, when ni (sky) turned up as preposition in Vedic, its nasalisation brought about 'to say negatively, scornfully'.

Vocabulary

ni = sky, ha = sound, ṣa = to be, ṭha = past (affix), la = mind, intellect, understanding ra = fire, to brighten.

17
Fruits from the Garden

va ṇa ṣa gha, va ga

The reading of this two-line text is doubtlessly correct.

The first three syllables va ṇa ṣa have fossilised in Vedic as vanas in vanas-pati (plant). This vanas also occurs outside compound (RV 10,172,1), but the meaning is uncertain. It is said to be derived from van but, if it is the fossilised form of va ṇa ṣa, the former itself should have been deduced from vanas. The Indus clause va ṇa ṣa means : through the waters (va) the plants (ṇa) grow (ṣa). The basic meaning of vanas should lie in 'water and plant'. Perhaps it expresses the tenderness of the young plant, and 'a tender feeling' (an abstract idea) is the intended sense. But its shorter form van is a concrete idea, referring to 'wood' (even 'tree'). Then śyeno ṇa vaṃsu sīdati (RV 9,57,3. 9,86,35) = Like a hawk sits in the wood (on the tree). Agni is called garbho vanām 'son of woods'. And, ā yāhi vanasā saha gāvaḥ sacanta vartaniṃ yad ūdhabhih = Come hither with a tender feeling, as cows have followed the path with udder.

The basic meaning of the deduced verb should be: to be tender or agreeable, to like or love.

The text quoted above means: Through the waters the plants will grow; irrigate the land (having these plants). The text relates to agriculture, horticulture in particular.

If the fourth syllable of the text precedes the third syllable, that is, if the text is va ṇa gha-ṣa, at the inflexional stage it would have become *va-ṇa gha-ṣa > vana k-sa > van ksa > var ksa > vra-ksa > vṛkṣa (tree).

The same text is preceded by ni  in another text. Then the meaning changes: ni va-ṇa ṣa-gha (oblique-case +s + v-future) = In the inhabited area (ni) the gardens (va- ṇa) will grow (ṣa-gha).

We should not be surprised to learn that they were engaged in agriculture with multifarious projects. Now, they were not required to collect fruits from the forests. They were cultivating gardens for fruits. In the post-Vedic Sanskrit literature we read that people used to have fruit gardens well-protected by the security agents.

18

A Hole on the Wall – A Symbolic Statement

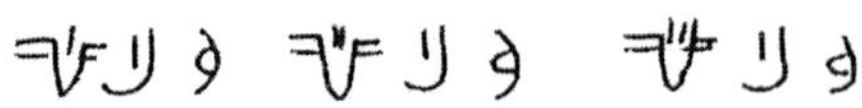

If there is a hole on the wall…

In the concordance of the Indus Script by Mahadevan, there are 25 texts which begin with ni nda ṣu, 8 texts which begin with ni nda si, and only 4 texts which begin with ni nda so. What these different vowels of the verb ṣa indicate is not clear, but commonly they suggest that the clause is syntactically related with the following clause in the text. That is to say, there is some conjunction like if, because, when, etc. at the head of the first clause.

Before we go to interpret these texts, we have to make some general observation on the language of the isolating type. A very controversial fact has to be stated that the language is not less than a living being, the phonemes being its body and their meanings being its breath to keep it alive. It moves just instinctively at this stage, following certain order in making the workable clauses. This instinctive language, like a plant or a primitive animal, at the so-called isolating stage in course of its evolution, is comprehensible only in a particular context just on the tongues of the speakers. As soon as the context changes, the meaning of the same clause changes abruptly. If such a language has been put to writing, its clauses may be comprehensible only when the context is known. And the context in the written text can be revealed only by the clauses accompanying the main clause. Now, even the field symbols accompanying the facts may be supposed to reveal the context or elaborate the text.

The language of the Indus inscriptions is such one. It has a body, full of life like the early beings of creation, but it has no mind. Its movement is instinctive.

In the interpretation of the Indus texts, we have to turn our mind to the remote countryside of India. Even the house of an affluent resident is badly lighted. It is dark even during the day, because there are no windows of the modern type. Near the roof of the house, there is a small circular or square hole to let the air and sunlight come. Having that situation in mind, we think that ni is the wall of the mud-built house, and nda is the hole near the roof. Thus ni nda ṣu means : if there is a hole on the wall.... The next clause  va ṇa ṭha says: in the house (va) the sunlight (ṇa) revolves (ṭha). This is the most primitive conception of the house-building engineering. In the early years of my childhood, I had enjoyed the luxury of such a house, which is no more available now.

The clause va ṇa ṭha has fossilised as vanád 'fire' in Vedic. When the sunlight enters the room through the air-hole, it appears to revolve. It looks like a beam of light.

2. In another text, the clause following ni nda ṣu is  la va ṇa ṭhi. The last three syllables va ṇa ṭhi has fossilised as varti 'the wick of a lamp' through *va na ti > *vanti > varti. In another context, we have noted that va ṇa ṭha has also otherwise fossilised as vanata > vanat > vart (vṛt) 'to turn round'. The revolving sunlight entering through the air-hole looks like the 'wick of a lamp'. Even va ṇa ṭhi should have meant 'in the house the sunlight revolves', but the verb turning towards i has made it a phrase 'the revolving sunlight in the house', ultimately giving it the meaning 'the wick of a lamp'.

The intrusion of la at the beginning of this clause suggests that it is in oblique case. If ra is for 'light', la may stand for a 'dark room'. la va ṇa ṭhi then means: in the dark room (there is) the wick of a lamp.

Now the whole text says: If there is hole on the wall, that is a lamp in the room.

3. In the text 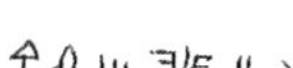 ni nda ṣu, ta na ṣa, the second clause ta na ṣa has fossilised as tánas 'offspring' which, however, appears to be irrelevant in respect to the first clause. But its further fossilisation as tars (tṛs) 'to be thirsty' seems to have to do with irrigation in agriculture. Perhaps giving waters to the thirsty land seems to be the point of reference. Then ta na ṣa seems to say: from the reservoir (ta = womb) canal (na) is dug out (to irrigate the agricultural land). The first clause slightly changes its meaning: if a hole is made in the embankment of the reservoir. The text perhaps intends to say: dig out canal from the reservoir

or the river and irrigate the land. Such little texts are likely to be the instructions of the civil administration of that primitive society. They had started agriculture and were devising various means to raise food crops.

4. In the text 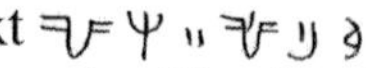 ni nda ṣu ka ṇa ṣa, the second clause ka ṇa ṣa has fossilised as *kanas > *kans > kars (kṛṣ) 'to plough land'. This refers to the agricultural activities. Here ka is 'water' and ṇa is 'earth'. Perhaps ka ṇa ṣa says: in the water till the land. The water makes the land soft and easy for tilling.
   The language at the isolating stage intends to say much more than what it actually says. The whole text seems to say: By making a hole in the embankment of river or reservoir, the water should be carried to distant land to make it easily ploughable. Such texts are generally accompanied by field symbols which reveal their intention.
5. The text  ni nda ṣu ta dha va-ga has two clauses following the main clause. When a hole has been made in the embankment of the reservoir, from the reservoir (ta) the waters rush out (dha, cf. dhāv) towards the land. Then va-ga advises: irrigate (va 'water' + ga 'injunction') the land. These little texts make us aware that they tried to exploit the gift of the nature properly and extensively. In a different text, we will see that ta dha means "the reservoir is full of waters". The full reservoir gives birth to a verb *tad 'to be full', which is the basis of tādurī 'pregnant' in the AV.
6. The text 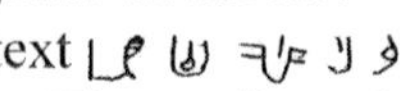 ni nda ṣu gā phū la has been discussed earlier. The reading of the second clause has been rectified. The meaning of the first clause also has little deviated. The syllable ni is the (wall of the) ear, and nda is the noise corresponding to the ear. Thus the first clause seems to say: If in the ear the sweet noise there is (= if some sweet noise is put in the ear). In the next clause, gā is an 'animal' in general and the 'cow/bull' in particular. The syllable phū stands for 'swoon' and la (time) stands for some idea corresponding to it. In modern dialects, phūl- is a verb meaning 'to swell' (as wound). Thus gā phū la means: the animal overcomes swoon. In the countryside, if an animal eats some poisonous plant, it fatally comes under swoon and recovers only when some loud noise is continuously poured into its ear. Thus the above text can be translated as follows: when the sweet sound is put into the ear, the animal overcomes

swoon. We know, however, that ni nda (the sweet sound in the ear) is the same as the later verb nind 'to scorn', the meaning making a frog's jump in the opposite direction.

7. In the text 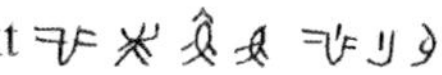 ni nda ṣu ma ni gra ṣa, the second part consists of four syllables.

As a rule, however, there are no four-syllabic clauses in the Indus texts. A three-syllabic text is either s + o + v or oblique case + s + v. Then there may be two clauses here: ma ni and gra ṣa. Because the verb of the first clause has turned towards i, it may be a phrase. Then ma-ni gra ṣa is the real clause, the phrase ma-ni being the subject and gra being the object of the verb ṣa.

In some village dialects, 'man' is a depression in the bed of the river, so that even when the river is thin in the dry season, this depression is deceptively and dangerously deep. Perhaps ma-ni means 'the water of the depression' or 'depression' itself.

The following syllables gra ṣa may have fossilised as gras 'to devour, eclipse, stop'. Now, ma-ni (s) gra (o) ṣa (v) seems to say: (the water of) the depression causes harm. If the main clause is prefixed, its meaning may change correspondingly: when a canal is dug out from the main river, the depression in the canal is dangerous.

This is a wise experience of the canal engineering of the primitive society.

8. ni nda ṣu da ṣa 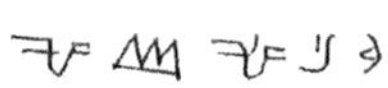

The reading and meaning of the first clause needs no elaboration. It has only to be clarified that the meaning "in the wall there is a hole" is symbolic, and it can point to anything relevant to the situation.

The first syllable of the second clause, namely da, requires an appropriate introduction to make this clause meaningful. In the Sanskrit lexicon of the monosyllabic words, da means 'mountain' along with other things. While the Avestan dahyu means 'village including its dwellers', the cognate Vedic dasyu means 'inhuman beings, unfriendly to mortals, demon, evil man, robber'. Bartholomae found it difficult to reconcile the Vedic and Avestan meanings due to misconceived Vedic ethnology. The modern Persian dih means 'village' and the pl. dihāt means the 'countryside'. As a matter of fact, da is the key to the original meaning, which remained unnoticed in the Avestan context. The word dasyu refers to a 'mountainous village' in the ur-Sanskrit. Even the cognate dāsa has the same meaning. As an ur-Sanskrit clause, it simply means: in the mountainous villages (da) they dwell (ṣa). The 'open' value of a has changed this Indus dasa into the Vedic Dāsa. The alternate form dasyu may have some deviating meaning on this line. Both Dāsa and Dasyu are connected with mountainous villages. Perhaps Dāsas were the permanent inhabitants and Dasyus were the fugitives who sought temporary shelter there. They were poor and uneducated people. Therefore, they resorted to theft and robbery. When chased by the dwellers of the urbanised areas, they took refuge in the hiding places of the mountainous villages. Those hiding places are called śārada-forts, literally meaning 'refuge-giving (*śāra = śaraṇa) places.

Now we should come to the Indus text. We can imagine a situation of the primitive people who had given up nomadic life and were settled in villages. When the villages were founded, the rogue elements appeared on the scene. They were called a-nās (ignorant and unwise), mṛdhra-vāk (rough-speaking) and kṛṣṇa-tvak (black-skinned) in the RV. When they entered the urban areas at night, they were chased away by the people and they took refuge in the hiding places of the mountainous villages.

With this background of the situation, the Indus text says: when there is hole in the wall, that is, when the rogue elements are physically spotted, in the mountains (da) they disappear (ṣa). The Dāsas and Dasyus were so-called because they used to run away and disappear in the mountainous villages. They were a-nās (ṇā = know + ṣa = see in the Indus text) 'ignorant and unwise'. They were mrdhra-vāk, because they spoke the uncultivated agglutinative ur-Sanskrit dialect. They were kṛṣṇa-tvak because they worked in the heat of the sun. They were neither non-Aryans nor inhuman and demonic, but only the outlawed groups of the Aryans.

The symbolic meaning of the clause ni nda ṣu shows how they had marched ahead in expressions even at the isolating stage of the language. We must change our views about the Aryans and Dravidians. They were Aryans and Dravidians at the same time.

The word draviḍa is a geographical term. Dra-mi-ḍa (later Dra-vi-ḍa) originally means: the (hot) sun (dra-, subj.) the country (mi-, obj.) makes hot (ḍa) = the hot sun makes the country hot, that is, the country of the hot sun. Dra > Ta- mi- ḍa > l = Tamil.

ni nda ṣu ca ra gā ḍa 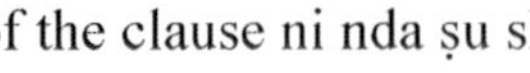

This polysyllabic text is somewhat unusual at the end. We know that there are only bisyllabic and trisyllabic clauses in the texts, but sometimes the division becomes difficult. Here the first three syllables make one clause, which is syntactically related with the following two bisyllabic clauses. The last two signs, however, are not doubtless as to their syllabic values.

The opening clause relates to the house-building engineering of the primitive society. It obviously means: when there are holes on the wall.... This context helps us to understand the immediately following bisyllabic clause ca ra. In the lexicons of the monosyllabic words ca means 'moon', which may also stand for the 'moon-light' in the present context. Then ra (fire, speed) may stand for its entry into the house and illumination. Thus ca ra seems to say: the moon-light enters the room and illuminates it. We can definitely say that the Sanskrit verb car 'to go, move' has phonetically evolved from it, though there may be other source for the meaning.

Taking for granted that the next two signs read gā ḍa, we try to interpret it. Though gāva (going into the stable) refers to the cow/bull, gā itself refers to the animals in general, perhaps even the little birds and other flying creatures (bees, wasps, etc.). More particularly, it refers to the undomesticated animals of the countryside, e.g. cats, ichneumons, monkeys, etc., which visit the human habitat without permission or invitation, usually from the wrong path, e.g. through the air-hole on the wall. They terrify the inmates of the house, specially the women and children. The syllable ḍa seems to express this idea, which is also inherent in the word ḍar 'fear'. Thus gā ḍa seems to say: the (intruding undomesticated) animals or creatures terrify (the house inmates).

Now the whole text may be put together: when there are holes on the wall, the moon-light enters and illuminates the room; (but) the undomesticated animals and the flying harmful creatures enter the room and terrify the house inmates.

The text points out that there are both benefits and disadvantages from the air-holes on the wall of the room. Though the moon-light illuminates the room, the undomesticated animals and the flying creatures may come through it and cause troubles. Therefore, one is advised to be careful about it. Perhaps taking note of this trouble, the air-holes were made very high on the wall, near the roof of the house. They were called gavākṣa (bull's eye) in Sanskrit. The little animals and the flying creatures do not dare to enter the house from that height.

9. ni nda ṣa ra ni nda ta ṇa 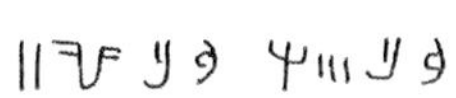

If the first two syllables (ni nda) make a phrase (a hole in the wall) and it is the subject, the third syllable may be the object and the fourth syllable may be the verb.

If ra (fire) means 'illuminates', ṣa (embryo) may stand for the internal space in the house. The whole text may have the following meaning: a hole in the wall illuminates the whole area. We have been going with this idea in several earlier texts. Even 'a hole' is just symbolic. It may be in plural.

The clause ni nda ta ṇa also does not mean anything else: ta (womb) may refer to the entire area inside the house and ṇa (light) may mean 'illuminates': a hole in the wall illuminates the entire area.

Of course, the type and the area of illumination may be different, because ṣa ra and ta ṇa are obviously different.

The Indus ṣa ra may have fossilised as sar (sṛ) and ta ṇa as tar (tṛ) in Vedic. Both these verbs are connected with 'movement', the first on the ground and the second on the water. Then the first relates to the lighting of the internal space on the moving vehicle and the second relates to the same on the boat.

Gradually we notice that, though at the isolating stage of the language, they had made tremendous advancement in technical knowledge. The wheeled carts and navigable boats had been invented and the domesticated animals drew the carts. Though the language looks clumsy and vague to us, it was a transparent vehicle of ideas for them, and they could express everything very intelligibly. Though there is no grammar at the isolating stage of the ur-Sanskrit, the phrases are formed by the coming together of two ideas expressed through two syllables.

10. ni nda ṣo pa śa, ci ẖa dhe ṣa 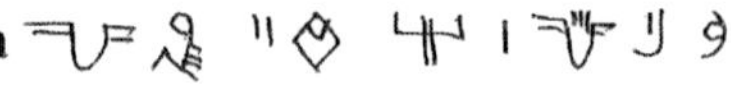

Apart from the fact that the last syllable of the opening clause ends with o, it is the same as in the previous texts with the verb in u. As such, it should not essentially differ from them in meaning. Thus it symbolically means: .... there is hole in the wall...

Even pa śa is not quite unfamiliar to us. It has been discussed in 'The early Indus civilisation' pp. 92-3 in connection with the text śa ma yo śa pa śa (no. 2369: Mahadevan). The clause pa śa is the seed of the Vedic verb paś-ya-ti (sees) and s-paś in s-paṣ-ṭa (clear, lit. seen physically), which is the extended form of paś through the prefixed s-. In that discussion, pa śa has been said to mean: see inside. It should mean: See the target (obj. +verb).

Before we come to the interpretation of ni nda ṣo pa śa, we have to go to the remote countryside in India and see the professional bird-hunter actually engaged in his work. He has a square or round curtain of straws and green leaves with a hole in the middle through which he can see the targeted birds. He besmears sticky substance on the pot containing grains of corn by which their feathers get stuck up and they cannot fly. The hunter then catches hold of them.

The text relates to that situation in the early stage of the human civilisation. Though they might have settled in villages, the hunting would have been one of their professions. The verb turned towards o seems to express the subjunctive idea. Therefore, the opening clause says: Let there be a hole in the curtain. The following clause naturally gives the instruction: (then) the target (pa) becomes visible (śa). It can also be translated thus: Make a hole in the curtain and see the target.

As there is no visible grammar in the language, it can he translated in many ways. Gradually we are realising that the diacritical marks on the syllables for specific vowels are always meaningful, which shows that the language was proceeding towards the agglutinative stage. We have already noted that some suffix elements had appeared; e.g. gha for future, ga for injunction, etc. Other affixes are just in our imagination on the basis of the later form of the language.

The same text continues in the second line with ci h̲a dhe ṣa. The clause ci h̲a has fossilised in Vedic as ca (and), probably through ci a > ca. With the affricate value of /c/, ci ha = tsi ha has fossilised as te (and) in Greek, and it is left with -h (and) alone in Gothic. It is surprising that 'and' is the uniform meaning in these three dialects of the ur-Sanskrit, and we must assume that this meaning is as old as the ur-Sanskrit. The meaning 'say' for ha is well-known, but ci is obscure as to its original meaning. Perhaps ci ha = to say it again.

The clause dhe ṣa has fossilised as dhiṣ in Vedic, and dhiṣ-ā means 'mindfully, zealously'. The meaning 'mind, thought' is apparent in dhe, and ṣa (wise) points to 'seeing'. Perhaps dhe ṣa means 'See through mind'.

Now the whole text may be translated: Let a hole be made in the curtain (ni nda ṣo), see (physically) the target (pa śa); and (ci h̲a = to say again) see through mind (dhe ṣa), that is, act carefully.

ni nda ṣu / so, ta gra ṣa 

11. Apart from the variation at the third syllable from the right side (ṣu : ṣo), there is no difference between the two texts. Therefore, they may be supposed to have essentially an identical meaning. It appears that the situation relates to the farming and the primitive water-engineering.

The first two syllables of the opening clause have close semantic correspondence with the first two syllables of the following clause: ni nda - ta gra. If ni is the river on this side of the text, ta is the 'artificial reservoir of waters' on the other side. If nda is the 'canal dug out from the main river', gra is the 'water rushing towards the reservoir'. Then we can propose the following translation: When the canal is dug out from the main river, the waters rush towards the reservoir. This is the meaning of the text with the first verb turned towards u (ni nda ṣu ta gra ṣa).

With respect to the second text with the first verb turned towards o, it can be said that it is an advice or instruction: Let a canal be dug out from the main river, so that the waters rush towards the reservoir.

The syllables ni nda of the first clause has fossilised as ninda- in the obscure compound ninda-tala 'having a fractured or broken hand'. The digging out of the canal reflects in the broken hand, because digging is a kind of violence inflicted on the earth.

The syllables ta gra of the second clause is perhaps traceable in the phonetically devoiced and semantically mutilated takra 'butter-milk', from which the verb tak has been deduced. How *tagra (the rushing of waters towards the reservoir) became takra 'butter milk' with a semantic jump requires thoughtful consideration, because 'butter milk' is as hygienic for a human being as the water is for the agricultural land. Also, the rushing of waters towards reservoir reflects very well in the verb tak 'to rush along' and its derivatives. A later word taṭāka (also taḍāga) contains ta- (reservoir) of the old vocable. With the preposition nis- the verb tak means 'to attack', which also reflects in the meaning 'to rush along'.

Thus we see that the Indus clauses reflect in the decomposed and stinking body of the Vedic vocables.

12. ni nda ṣo ni ha śa ma yo ṣa 

The opening clause ni nda ṣo is an instruction or advice: Dig out a canal from the main river. We should take note of the fact that, though still primitive, it was an agrarian society but proceeding towards urbanisation. It briefly explains the benefits of the canal system. There are three bisyllabic clauses: ni ha śa ma yo ṣa.

The second and third clauses have fossilised as śam yos, and they are used jointly (saṃ yoḥ) as well as severally (saṃ ca yoś ca) in the RV. As clauses, they mean: let evil (śa) end (ma); let comfort (yo) be there (ṣa). The fossil śam is used as the first member of a compound (in śaṅkara, śambhu, etc.), though yos has ceased to exist in Sanskrit.

The clause ni ha has fossilised as nih (AV 2,6,5. VS 27,6), which is explained as ni-hantṛ (killer) by Mahīdhara and is proposed by Roth to be emended as nid. Both Mahīdhara and Roth are unacceptable, though Roth is semantically nearer to the intended meaning. As nid has been extensively used elsewhere, the Vedic singers might have been aware of their semantic identity, though nih was already on the death-bed in the AV.

There is some ground to assume that nid and nih, though originally different, are identical semantically. They are equivalents, ha means 'sky', the chief quality of which is 'sound' (śabdaikaguṇa ākāśaḥ). Therefore, ha also means 'sound', and we see it in āha (said). Even /d/ has 'sound' as one of the meanings, as we see in gad (to speak distinctly), nad (to make indistinct noise), vad (to speak in human voice), etc. Even Latin dire (to say) is comparable. Therefore, nih and nid are two words with identical meaning. If ni ha means 'in the sky (ni) it sounds (ha)', it may be equal to 'People say'. Thus the text says: Dig out canal from the main river. People say: the hardship will end. There will be comfort.

By the time of the Vedas, 'people say' would have deteriorated in meaning because of ni-, which had become a preposition with some negative meaning. Thus niha would have begun to mean 'to say negatively', 'to scorn, to censure'. The same was the fate of nid, which survived in the language nevertheless.

13. ni nda ṣu la ṣa 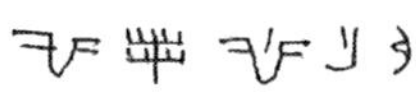

Even if the meaning of the opening clause is almost properly understood, it is supposed to be modified by the meaning of the following clause.

Only the fossilised form of the Indus clause in Vedic can guide us towards the intended meaning of the Indus clause, because a language without grammar is a creature without mind, which moves only instinctively. That is to say, a language at the isolating stage is just an animal and we have very little idea about its intention.

Hypothetically, we assume that the following clause la ṣa would have fossilised as *rasa > *ṛṣa, from which the verb ṛṣ would have been deduced. The meaning 'to flow, flow quickly' appears to be genuine, but the meaning 'to push, thrust' is just derived. This deduced root ṛṣ is also extended as v-ṛṣ, and in vṛṣ-an 'bull', the flow of liquid has turned metaphorical. But 'to flow quickly' also reflects in the Indus clause. The clause la ṣa means: the waters rush forth. Then the opening clause seems to say: even if there is a little rupture in the embankment (of the river or reservoir), the waters rush forth quickly.

This appears to reflect the experiences of the Indus civil administration looking after agriculture. They warn the people about the safety of the embankment, so that not a drop of water goes waste.

The word ṛṣi 'seer' also originally relates to this ṛṣ, who lets his thoughts rush out quickly from his mind. Even the mantra are said to 'resemble the showers of the rain-cloud' (abhrād vṛṣṭir ivājani).

14. ni nda ṣu ta dha, va ga 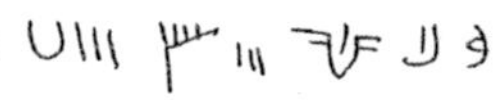

Only the central part of the text, ta dha, seems to need explanation. The first part, ni nda ṣu, means: when there is a hole in the wall. This meaning is symbolic, which may be adapted to any situation. Here it suggests the inflow of the water in the reservoir from outside. This would have further suggested the 'mating of the pair' in the Atharvavedic culture.

ta dha is a clause. Its fossilised form in Vedic is not available, but the AV (4,15,14) has preserved a very obscure vocable tādurī (also taduri in 15). It is in the voc. sg. form tāduri, being the adjective of maṇḍūkī 'a female frog'.

All the proposed etymologies and meanings from Yāska to Monier-Williams are hypothetical. The word tādurī may be obviously derived from some verb *tad, which may be the deaspirated form of *tadh from the Indus phrase or lexeme *tadha. The meaning of tāduri may throw some light on the Indus clause ta dha.

The AV stanza (4,15,14) reads:

> upa pra vada maṇḍūki varṣam ā vada tāduri,
> madhye hradasya plavasva vigṛhya caturaḥ padaḥ

'Speak forth sweetly, o female frog; address (your desire) to the rain, o tāduri; swim in the middle of the pond, expanding the four legs'.

Here the female frog is addressed as tādurī. The pādas c-d of the stanza are suggestive of some joy. What may be the cause of that joy? The female frog is perhaps pregnant; she has a foetus in the womb. In the Indus text, [ta = womb and dha = dhatte (contains, is full of)], ta dha seems to say: the reservoir is full (of waters). When the clause ta dha contracted as phrase and was finally a lexeme, *tad was deduced from *tadha, which meant 'to keep in womb, conceive, be pregnant'. Thus tādurī means 'pregnant'.

The full Indus text then says: when, through the embankment (ni) there is in-flow (nda) of waters, the reservoir (ta) is full (dha) or filled up; irrigate (the land through it).

The primitive pastoral Idea went on floating till it reached the AV period. The in-flow of waters and the fullness of the reservoir turned into conceiving. Giving birth to a vocable tādu-rī, the verb tad itself disappeared from the language.

The gap of time between the two texts (Indus inscriptions : AV) is so great that no exact correspondence may be established. The ideas of the Indus texts have gone many transformations by the time of the AV. The 'fullness of the reservoir with waters' (tadha) may have shifted to 'containing something inside', then to 'being pregnant'. When the verb tad 'to conceive' was deduced and a derivative tādurī 'pregnant' was formed, it disappeared from the language.

19

sas 'to be lazy'

sa ṣi ta dha

sa ṣi may have fossilised as sas, occurring several times in the RV and AV. It means 'to sleep', 'to be inactive'. Its derivatives sasa and sasya, however, mean 'grass', probably because it is in lying down state on the earth.

In the lexicons, ṣa means 'fence'. Then ṣa ṣi seems to say: if there is a fence. It is not an ordinary statement. It refers to some strong structure, a strong embankment.

If ta dha is the same as suggested by tādurī (pregnant), it may mean: the reservoir is full.

The whole text now says: If there is a fence, that is, if the embankment is strongly structured, the reservoir is always full of waters.

We may notice, how the strong structure needing no repair for a long time has semantically degenerated into 'slumber' and 'laziness'.

20
āha 'said'

ā ha (past-say = said)

This two-sign text is a little hard nut to crack. The second from the right is easily recognisable as ha, being the numeral sign. But the first from the right is clue-less about its identity. Its simpler graphic form is o-o, pictographically the two eyes of an animal.

In Sanskrit, an 'eye is akṣi/akṣa/akṣan. If the first syllable a- was for 'eye' in the ur-Sanskrit, and if there was a clause *a-ka-ṣa meaning 'in-the-eye' (a) 'light' (ka) 'there-is' (ṣa), which later contracted as a-ka-ṣa > akṣa, we can presume that o-o is a and  is ā. Unfortunately, the first sign in the combination -kaṣa is damaged, so that our hypothetical a-ka-ṣa remains hypothetical.

About the meaning of ā in the ur-Sanskrit, there are only secondary references. In Sanskrit dramas, an actor suddenly exclaims: ā smarāmi (O yes, I remember). By this, we may imagine that ā refers to the past, because 'remembering' is associated with past.

At the agglutinative stage of the ur-Sanskrit, ā-ha could be assumed to mean past-say, but shortly before, it could have indicated 'in-the-past' (ā) 'one said' (ha).

21
The Sign for Cha

This sign may be phonetically identified as cha. If O is ca, ꝏ may be cha by a simple imagination. From the meaning of some Sanskrit words beginning with /ch/, we may assume that cha is something which covers, which is spread over an area, that is, a shade, shelter, bower, shadow. Even 'smallness' is suggested: cha-ga 'goat' literally means 'small-horned'; chi shows disgust; and cho means 'to cut'. It cannot be guessed with what meaning this cha was added to i-, ga- ya- , pra- , ra- in the pre-historic stage of Sanskrit. Perhaps it intensified the idea of the previous syllable.

In its single occurrences, it is perhaps some 'shelter' for the wandering men in that primitively urbanised society. It would have been a traveller's inn, hut, cottage. No clause containing this cha has fossilised in the later language. But in the rustic dialects of the countryside, there is an injunctive form ha-ga meaning 'do defecate', which seems to form a part of the following Indus clause; ha ga cha ṣa gha. If the first part means as said above, the second part seems to say: the smell (cha) is there (ṣa) indeed (gha). cha meaning 'smell' may be deduced from the colloquial chi showing disgust. Though that complex was bad-smelling, one was advised to use it. It was a sign-board of that complex.

The text || ⊨) ꝏ cha ppa ra has been read so on the basis of the modern colloquial chappar 'the thatched roof of a house'. If this reading is correct, the graphic doubling of the consonant pa is remarkable. The text as a clause seems to say: for a shade (hut or cottage) use straws and leaves. This might be the easiest and cheapest form of making a shelter for the people going from one place to another in that primitive society. Gradually cha had acquired associated meanings.

From the Vedic language we know that the people had several types of houses, namely: da-ma, which literally means 'the suffering ends' (a very comfortable house); vanar in vanar-gu and - sad from va ṇa ra (in the dwelling animals go); and ama in the adv. amā (in the house) from ẖa ma ha (the house gives comfort), cognate with Eng. home, German Heim.

There are some other texts:

Ga cha ṣa = the tree gives shade, the tree is a temporary shelter. Perhaps its first part has fossilised as gāch (a shady tree), = chāyā-druma in the literary language.

Cha ra ṣa = the hut is comfortable. va ga = Dwell in it.

Cha ra = A comfortable hut. Through the affricate value of ch we may imagine a Vedic verb śṛ in śar-ad 'autumn' (a pleasant season) śar-aṇa 'refuge', śar-man 'peace'. The śārada forts of the Dāsas and Dasyus of the RV may be connected with it. It was a safe fort.

la cha ṭha va ga

This text appears to be a little more intelligible. If la undergoes rhotacism, cha splits as affricate and ṭha becomes t or d in Vedic, the fossilised *raśad or *raśat is the result, but that is unquotable. However, a root *raś seems to come out, which we have in raś-mi, raśanā, etc. The Indus text says: Turn la (the tape) around cha (the back of the horse) and ride. Perhaps the domestication of the horse is the point of reference.

22
sakṣ 'to be strong'

pa ma na śa na, sa ka ṣa

The reading of the text should not be doubted, even though the sound-values of some signs are not confirmed. Because each syllable is a word, any combination could make a bisyllabic or a longer word in the later phase of the language.

The clause sa ka ṣa of the second line has contracted as sakṣa adj. of disputable meaning. From this sakṣa, a verb sakṣ of uncertain meaning seems to have been deduced, which makes the participle sakṣat (RV 1,131,3) and two derivatives sakṣaṇa and sakṣaṇi (RV). They are not quite certain as to their meanings.

The last two syllables śa na of the first line have come together in Vedic as śaṇa 'a kind of hemp', because n and ṇ differed only phonetically, not phonemically, in the ur-Sanskrit, and colloquially ṇa was more favoured than na. Phonetically, śaṇa is not different from the Greek kannabis, and even hemp is not widely different, coming through the Germanic source. This śaṇa has yellowish white fibre, from which strings are made.

The first two syllables have been read pa ma (which may be disputed), and, with the third read na, they become pa ma na, which is not traceable in Sanskrit in any fossilised form. The first syllable may be pa, because it refers to a plant, and ma value for the second is guaranteed from elsewhere. Therefore, even arbitrarily, we may read it pa ma na. In the modern dialect, the plant is called paṭuā, which retains the first syllable.

Before we take up the interpretation of the Indus text, we must take note of a cottage industry in the remote villages of the countryside. The plant paṭuā is grown in the rainy season. When mature, it is uprooted and thrown in the waters in bundles. The outer skin of the plant is dissolved in water and white shining fibres come out, from which strings are made by twisting them in small bunches.

With this background, we may interpret the text. Pa is the plant itself. Ma may be the resin. na means 'to shine'. pa ma na = In the plant (pa) the resin (ma) shines (na). That is to say, there is shining resin in the stem of the plant. śa na = the fibre shines. That is to say, the resin becomes fibres. sa means snake, and its zigzag movement suggests the twisting or winding action. When ka + ṣa contracted as k-ṣa, sakṣa was analysed in Vedic as sah + ṣa, the verb sah 'to conquer, overpower', reflecting the meaning of ka as 'power, strength'. Thus ṣa ka ṣa = twisting makes strong. That is to say, when the fibres are twisted, a strong rope comes out.

Now we can examine the meanings of the derivatives of sakṣ. Because sakṣa was analysed as sah + ṣa, the meaning 'to conquer, overpower' itself runs through all the derivatives, and Geldner is right in sticking to this meaning in all the passages. Because it could also be analysed as sac + ṣa, Roth has also suggested the meaning 'to accompany'. The Vedic singers had always perhaps only sah in their mind.

23
The Milk is Hygienic

ma ṣa ma yo ṣa

A very usual Indus text śa ma yo ṣa, consisting of two bisyllabic clauses śa ma and yo ṣa, has been extended by ma at the beginning. This trick, then, makes two trisyllabic clauses: ma śa ma and ma yo ṣa. The isolating type of the language is itself very brief in making statements, but this trick shows that the people were very enlightened in the use of their language even at the isolating stage. Moreover, a primitive community is supposed to change its vocabulary as soon as it changes its habitation. The first ma of the text is not the same as the third ma. Therefore, they have changed the signs.

The original text śa ma yo ṣa seems to say: Let the misery (or illness) end; let the comfort (or recovery) be there. This is the wishful thinking of that primitive community. These two clauses have fossillised as śam yos (wellbeing and comfort) in Vedic. The syllable ma added at the beginning of the text seems to refer to 'milk', and then the clauses appear to say: the milk restores health/through the milk there is recovery from illness; the milk gives strength. Out of the second clause ma yo ṣa, the first two syllables have become a part of the Vedic compounds mayo-bhu, mayo-bhuva, -bhava meaning healthy, hygienic.

This text seems to suggest that the milch cattle had begun to be domesticated. The part mayo- in the compound was supposed to be due to sandhi and, thus, a new vocable mayas was conceived. This word, however, became obsolete later.

When all the Indus texts are read, a large number of the underivable Vedic words may be identified and their meanings determined.

24
And Smell Through Nose

ci ẖa ṇa ṣa

The clause ci ẖa na ṣa has been used a number of times in the Indus texts, singly (291 times) as well as in combination. As a plain clause it seems to say: Speak truly: an advice or order. As a phrase, at the beginning of another clause it means: truly said, to tell the truth, and similar ideas. Through it one gives advice, order, etc. Just as every Vedic stanza, starts with OM (and its intended meaning is not known), many Indus texts begin with ci ẖa, as if the following advice has to be taken note of.

It has also to be noted that ci ẖa has phonetically contracted, as ca in Vedic, que in Latin, (through the affricate value of c) as te in Greek and Punjabi, and as -h in Gothic. Everywhere it means 'and'. Its phonetic contraction is as remarkable as its semantic change.

The clause following ci ẖa is na ṣa, which seems to give order or advice or injunction. Its meaning has to be determined.

The clause na ṣa would have become the phrase nasa with the same body of syllables at the later stage, and fossilised as nas in Vedic, where it means 'nose'. As the first syllable itself generally retains the original meaning, at the isolating stage of Indus, nas perhaps referred to 'nose' in the human body. The following ṣa is the verb, and its meaning is some activity related with nose.

From nás a verb nas too (meaning 'to smell') would have been deduced. In Vedic nas means 'to join'. Perhaps the two holes of the nose are supposed to be joined, though nas has other meanings too. In Germanic languages, this nas is preceded by ge- (German genesen 'to recover from illness, to give birth to a child'). The verb nas seems to have given birth to *nāsaka 'smeller', from which there is the f. form nāsikā 'nose'.

With reference to ṇa meaning 'nose', ṣa may mean 'to smell' 'snuff', 'sniff'; na ṣa = (Please) smell through the nose. It is an advice. While tasting some food for eating, it should be examined. If it smells bad, it should not be eaten. With reference to na meaning 'illness' ṣa means 'to recover': na ṣa = May (the person) recover from illness 'Giving birth to a child' of German 'genesen' reflects in ṣa meaning 'embryo'. This sense can be derived if na ṣa means something like this: take out from the river.

The speech of a primitive community has a different meaning as the situation changes. Thus in ci ẖa na ṣa, both ci ẖa and na ṣa may have different meanings according to the changing habitations of those nomadic people.

25

gha ṇa

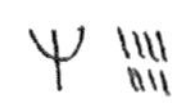

gha ṇa (The sun is becoming hotter day by day)

This two-sign text, with the elephant as a field symbol, reads gha ṇa, which is doubtless. Its meaning too is hardly doubtful. Briefly it only says: the sun is hot. But the relevance of the text has to be properly explained. The field symbol accompanying this text too has to be justified.

For the Eng. 'day', Germ. 'Tag', etc. the reconstructed IE form is dhagha, which may be supposed to mean: the hot sun. As a clause, it could mean: the sun is hot. It also reflects in Skt. dah 'to burn', nidāgha 'summer', in the modern colloquial dāg 'to inflict by fire'. It is also a Santhali verb meaning 'to cremate a dead body'. The day is so-called because it is hot and shining. That is to say, gha = sun, and ṇa = hot or shining is possible.

The phrase ghaṇa may easily have given birth to the verb ghar-, because n has changed into r in many cases; e.g. sarvan > sarvar-ī. From the verb ghar-, we have the derivatives like ghar-ma (1. fire 2. sun 3. heat 4. kettle 5. heated offering 6. flame), ghṛ-ṇa (heat, glow), ghṛ-ṇi (sun-rays) and ghṛ-ta (clarified butter). If these phonetic connections are doubtless, the meaning of gha ṇa as stated above may be reasonable.

The relevance of the text may lie in the context of the Indus agriculture. The Indus people were in the early stage of farming. Though they had mostly to depend on the monsoon for the waters, they may also have devised other means of irrigation. But their language was such as it could not fully express what they intended to say. Therefore, much was left on the wisdom and understanding of the people and on the field symbols.

As the sun was becoming hotter day by day, they were expecting the snow to melt on the Himalayas and abundance of waters flowing in the snow-fed rivers. The people were advised to store as much waters as possible for the fields and reservoirs. They did not like that even a drop of waters should escape to the sea.

Here the field symbol 'elephant' signified the expected black rain-clouds of the coming monsoon, predicting good crops and prosperity. It also suggested abundance of waters in the rivers. The trunk suggested storing waters for distribution to the fields.

The field symbols were not connected with the literal meanings of the texts, because the same text has different field symbols and the same field symbol has different texts. The field symbols have symbolic meanings, which can be presented in a whole paragraph. The field symbols may be initially distinguished as good and bad. Then, among the good and bad, there may be various gradations. The elephant, bull, etc. are symbols of good intention.

The Indus people were the speakers of the ur-Sanskrit at the isolating stage. Though they had attained material prosperity and intelligence of mind, their language was not growing with the same speed. They were employing the language beyond its capacity. Because they were intelligent people, they invented a way to make their intention clear by adding field symbols to the text. Naturally, the field symbols suggested much more than what could be said by words. The field symbols are actually cartoon to the algebrical Indus texts.

Thus we can say that the Indus texts are presented in two languages - verbal and symbolic. The one was audible, the other was suggestive. The field symbols explained the texts in manner which no commentary could do.

26
Text no. 1623/2847

lu bha dhī ṣa ṭha ga ga ga ṇa
ya gha ṣu bra sī cha ra
ṣu ṇa ga ci ra ḍha ṇa ta gra ṣa

This long text consists of 9 + 7 + 10 = 26 signs in three lines, and appears twice in this small corpus of texts. Many small texts appear several times due to their propagandist contents, but this longest text appearing twice makes us think about its relevance. Let us examine what this text intends to say, though some signs are even graphically uncertain, while some others, though phonemically identified, are uncertain as to meanings.

The first sign is l- with some vowel. Because the following sign stands for bha (sky), the first sign may be read lu, which, reflect in the Vedic lubh 'to be foggy'. The first syllable lu is associated with fogginess and qualifies bha in some oblique case. The third syllable dhī (light) is the subject of ṣa-ṭha, the verb 'be' in the past tense. Thus the first part of the first line –lu bha dhī ṣa-ṭha – says: In the foggy sky, there was light.

The following syllable ga (star) has been repeated thrice to show plurality, and the verb ṇa naturally means 'to twinkle'. Thus, ga ga ga ṇa = The stars were twinkling. This justifies why there was light in the foggy sky. This whole clause has squeezed as the noun gagana (sky).

In the second line, the verb of the first clause is bent towards u, which shows that it is dependent on the next two bisyllabic clauses. Though the graphically uncertain ya is also uncertain semantically, the following gha (sun) suggests that it refers to 'the other side of the horizon'. The next two bisyllabic clauses, bra sī and cha ra, are uncertain both graphically and semantically. But the si value of the bird-sign is suggested by the preceding (also graphically uncertain) bra reflecting in bṛsī. If sī means 'to fly', bra is certainly for the birds in general, reflecting in the old Eng.

Brid from the Germanic source. Thus bra sī = The birds were flying (back into their nests). On the other hand, ra (play) of the next clause suggests that cha refers to the 'owl' (because it finds pleasure in darkness). Cha ra = The owls were playing (in the darkness). The whole second line says: Because the sun was on the other side of the horizon, (it was already the sunset) all the birds were retiring to their nests, while the owls were playing in the open sky.

The third line is the longest. The first two syllables, ṣu and ṇa, are either two verbs or constitute a bisyllabic verb ṣu-ṇa, followed by the injunctive affix -ga. Colloquially, sunaga is itself an injunctive form, meaning 'please listen-to'. Many obscure clauses and phrases of this type are still current in the village dialects. One, e.g., of them is kī do (they say that...). Ci ra = A long time passed. ḍha (sound) ṇa (light). Ci ra ḍha ṇa = For a long time, there was thundering and lightning. Ta gra ṣa = In the womb the sun went. That is to say, the sun disappeared in the darkness of the night. The gist of the whole third line is: It was a dreadful dark night with thundering and lightning for a long time. Colloquially, there is ḍhan-ḍhan which only refers to a confused sound.

This is the message of this little paragraph of nearly ten clauses and phrases. Naturally it generated fear and superstition among the general mass. We also see the wild adventure of this primitive language, which endeavours to describe an event even beyond its capacity. The broken pieces of this primitive language is scattered not only in the Vedic language but also in the village dialects of today. Because it was a long text, no field symbol was required. The field symbols accompany only the small texts.

27
The Earliest Text Reinterpreted

It was in 1997 that I was able to read, first of all, an Indus text 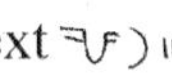 as ta na ṣa. I interpreted it, on the basis of the traditional Sanskrit lexicons of the monosyllabic words, as follows: from the womb (of a woman) gems come out. That is to say, the children born from the womb of women are gems. It was the result of an arduous labour for the last three years. The lead to this success was the identification of the Indus numeral script, meticulously arranged in specific order, with the syllabic order of the Māheśvara-sūtras at the beginning of the Pāṇini's grammar. The first two signs from the right are numerals. The last sign, an animal figure, was identified as ṣa through a different approach. Later, the same text was found in three other graphic forms; they are 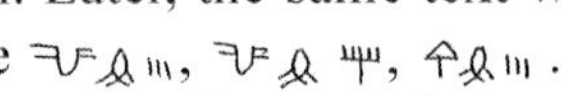. It appeared that three types of script have been employed in the Indus texts:

Sound	Animal figure	Geometrical figure	Numeral
ta			
na			
ṣa			

It is seen that there is no text exclusively in one type of script. The animal variety of ta and the geometrical variety of na is also otherwise not definitely identifiable. Of course, there is a single text  śa pha ja exclusively in animal figures, probably the earliest text, when the geometrical figures and numerals were not invented.

The above meaning of the text was reached on the basis of its reduced form tánas 'offspring' in the RV (5,70,4). But now it appears that this meaning of the text had been conceived much later, on the threshold of the inflexional stage of the language, when the Indus society had become sophisticated and the ethical concepts had begun to emerge. At an earlier stage of the language, we do not expect such a refined ethical idea. Though they were no more hunters, had settled in villages, engaged in ordinary form of agriculture, seeing gem in child envisages a much advanced level of culture. It is, however, also supposed that at the lowest level of the society, the isolating stage of the ur-Sanskrit was also limping ahead.

It is said that the vocabulary of the primitive communities changed after every generation. All the monosyllabic words of the clause ta na ṣa would have started with crude meanings, referring to physical objects of very ordinary experience, e.g. mountains, rivers, lakes and natural ponds, etc. We may give below the various transformations of the imaginary meanings of the isolating clause ta na ṣa:

1. From the mountain (ta) the waters (na) flow (ṣa).
2. From the main river (ta) canals (na) are dug out (ṣa).
3. From the reservoirs (ta) canals (na) are dug out (ṣa).
4. From the womb (reservoir) waters come out.
5. From the womb (of a woman) gems (like children) come out.

Almost on the threshold of the inflexional stage of the language, when the monosyllabic words were rapidly dying out and the clauses consisting of the monosyllabic words were becoming obsolete, specially at the upper level of the society, the traditional lexicographers had begun to collect the monosyllabic words. They found the meanings of the syllables reflecting in the Vedic words. Then ta = womb, na = gem, ṣa = embryo.

Even now the rustic dialects of the remote villages in India preserve the monosyllabic Indus words. In one story, it is said: Our Guru is coming with the limping ṭa (leg) of a bitch. na for 'no' and ta for 'yes' is common.

Thus we suppose that ta na ṣa would have travelled through all the imaginary meanings stated above.

This ta na ṣa text is elsewhere extended by bha at the beginning and gha at the end: bha ta na ṣa gha 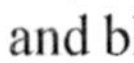. Evidently, gha at the end is the future affix attached with the verb ṣa, and bha at the beginning may be an adjective qualifying the oblique-case ta.

If na refers to a canal, ta may be the main river or reservoir. The adjective bha in association with ta may have the meaning 'full' or 'over-flooded'. The possible meaning of the extended clause may be: From the full or over-flooded river or reservoir canals will be dug out.

Bha ta na may have turned into a phrase (= a canal from the over-flooded reservoir) and its benefits would have been realised. Phonetically, the central ta between two voiced sounds would have been voiced to da (bha da na). At the inflexional stage, the accent on the last syllable would have weakened the central vowel and the nasal would have undergone rhotacism: bha-d-ra 'pleasing, shining, beautiful, good'. The original n may be still traceable in the verb bhand. The development of the meanings of bhadra in Vedic is remarkable, but not improbable.

The text ta na ṣa is accompanied by the field symbol of a unicorn. It is a mischievous beast and very ungrateful, knowing no friendship or acquaintance. Even a lion or tiger may be friendly to its caretaker, but not this beast. It seems to be suggested by this field symbol that the river coming from the mountain or even the canal dug out from the main river or reservoir, though beneficial for agriculture and for the people at large, may be dangerous. The manger put before the beast suggests that there should be some control on the flow of the river.

A whole paragraph can be written on the suggestiveness of this field symbol. The angle of its face and horn may be suggestive in some way or other. The form of the manger also differs as we pass from the unicorn to the bison, rhinoceros and tiger, and the same is absent in case of Zebu, buffalo and elephant.

28
The Seven Rivers of the Punjab

The RV often refers to seven rivers (e.g. 1,35,8), but the whole region of the Punjab is comprehended through the modern five rivers, namely: Jhelum, Chenab, Sutlej, Rabi and Beas. In the list of the seven rivers, certainly, the dried up Sarasvatī and the outlying Sindhu are included.

The language of the Indus inscriptions is primitive to the extent that anything could be described only through a clause, not through a name, though some syllables may have stood for certain rivers. The river, later called Sarasvatī, was mightily flowing before them, but the speakers of the language of the Indus texts simply observed: ṣa ra ṣa = from-the-mountain flows (and) stops (at the sea). When the clause ṣa ra ṣa was contracted and reduced to sáras 'pond, lake', which highlighted the whole bed of the river, it was called Saras-vat-ī 'consisting of ponds or lakes'. But then it was the Vedic language. Generally, the initial word or syllable becomes a part of the whole name.

Even Sindhu is the Vedic name, only known to the Vedic people who conceived it to 'flow stealthily', deriving it from syand, with Samprāsaraṇa on the first syllable and aspiration on the last consonant. The older generation of the Vedic people, that is, the Indus people, perhaps did not know it by the present name. How they described it, as in the case of Sarasvatī, we do not know. We hear of a mythical river Rasā in the RV, but whether it was Sindhu we cannot say. The name rasā is an agglutinative formation: ra (flow) sa (shake-wise) = Flows in a zigzag way.

The naming of the river Gaṅgā is much later, evidently derived from gam 'to go' without the palatalisation on the first syllable. This name was conceived at a time when the palatalisation of the reduplicated guttural had stopped.

The names of the other five of the seven rivers of the RV, namely Asiknī (Jhelum), Vitastā (Chenab), śutudrī (Sutlej),Vipāśā (Beas) and

Puruṣṇī (Rabi) are pre-Vedic, as appearing from the outer look of the words. They should have been in the form of clauses at the isolating stage of the ur-Sprache.

It appears that the clauses of the isolating stage themselves have contracted and become Vedic names. These names may be analysed on the Vedic pattern to arrive at their clause forms.

If Puruṣṇī is analysed as puru + ṣṇī on the Vedic pattern, puru- being cognate with the Gk. poly- (many) and -snī not very different from snā 'to bathe', it may be understood as 'having many streams'. At the clause stage, pu ru snī may have meant : through (the river) pu irrigate the land. It was an instruction to the farmers. Even snā 'to bathe' is a combination of sa and na, just as nada- (avyakte śabde) is a combination of na 'to flow' and da 'to make indistinct noise.

Similarly, the last syllable drī of śutudrī is not different from dra 'to run'. If tu stands for 'sea', śu tu drī means: (the river) śu rushes towards sea.

If Asiknī is analysed as asi + knī, asi (sword) may suggest a straight course of the river. The verb kni may reflect in kri. Perhaps the clause a si kni means: this (river) flows straight.

The last two syllables of Vipāśā suggest that this river was seen joining the bigger Sutlej. As a clause, it could have meant: this river (vi) joins another river (pa).

In Vitastā, vi is the river, ta is the sea, and sta represents the verb sthā. This clause seems to say: this river stops at the sea.

By the interpretation of these names, we come to the conclusion that some syllables were also the names of the rivers: śu = śutudrī, vi = Beas and Chenab, pu = Rabi.

The basis of the modern names of the five rivers is not known. Because the old names appeared to be outdated, new names from the vernaculars were coined for them.

29
Some Sacrificial Formulas

ṛc, vauṣaṭ, nakta

This text in two lines consists of three bisyllabic clauses with the verb (ṣa) in the past tense, common for all the three subjects. That is to say, the full clauses appear to be the following: ra ca ṣa-ṭha, va u ṣa-ṭha, ṇa ka ṣa-ṭha.

Though the isolating stage of a language is itself laconic in form, its further abbreviation here is remarkable. They may be said to mean as follows: there was blaze in the fire, there was coldness in the water, there was light in the sky.

Perhaps some natural situation or even a catastrophic event is described. The past tense has been employed, but that may be meant for some recurring situations.

The first clause without the verbal part may have fossilised as ṛc, as we have in arcis 'flame'. The third clause along with the verbal part may have fossilised as nakta 'night' < nak-s-ta < na ka s-ta < na ka ṣa-ṭha. Though the night is ordinarily dark, its original conception was that of a star-lit (bright) night. Its synonym rātrī is originally 'illuminator' < rā + tṛ + ī. Even elsewhere, we have seen that nag < ṇa ga means: the light has gone away, that is, the darkness has come. It is only negatively that the night is conceived as dark in Sanskrit.

The second clause va u is difficult to be traced, unless vauṣaṭ is the contracted form of the whole clause va u ṣa ṭha.

We have any how reached the fossilised forms of the three clauses, but the relevance of this text for that primitive society is still obscure.

Vocabulary

ra = fire ca = blaze va = water u = coldness ka = light na = sky.

30
The acc. pl. gās

The Vedic acc. pl. gā-s 'cow/bull'

The following two texts are not identical, but the first two and the fourth signs are the same in each text:

ni nda ṣu ga pha la 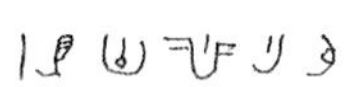
ni nda si ga ka ṣa 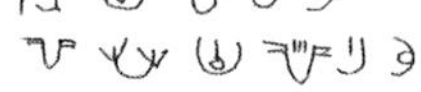

The reading of the first three signs in each line is still unconfirmed, and the reading of the fourth is equally so. Provisionally, it is gā. We know it as a verb in the clause gā va (goes into-the-stable). In the phrase gāva (going into the stable) the verbal idea is still present, but in the lexeme gāva 'cow/bull' it is not even imaginable, though the traditional Sanskrit grammarians saw the verbal idea alone in go- (gacchatīti gauḥ).

What we may read gā va  in the middle of some long Indus texts occurs more than 100 times, where it appears to be a lexeme rather than a clause or phrase. As 'cow' was the first milch cattle to be domesticated, gā va is not likely to appear as a phrase or clause in the Indus texts. By the time of the writing of the Indus texts, gāva was certainly a word for 'cow', domesticated long ago. By the time of Patañjali, gāva had also developed a fem. form gāvī in the colloquial speech.

In the present two texts, gā occurs alone, but it is equal to gāva, because the Vedic acc. pl. form gās shows the base gā-. We have elsewhere interpreted the line ni nda ṣu gā pha la thus: When in the ear (ni) the sweet sound (nda) is produced (ṣu), the cow (gā) overcomes the swoon (pha la). The last two syllables reflect in the word phala (fruit), which is etymologically still doubtful. The vowel i or u with the verb in the first clause seems to have the same function, namely to show that the two clauses are related. The second line seems to say: When the sweet sound is produced in the ear, the cow (gā) gives milk (ka ṣa). That is to say, the cow gives milk on hearing a sweet sound.

The last two syllables ka ṣa seems to reflect in kṣī-ra[1] 'milk', though it itself is the abbreviated form of some other clause. The word kṣma for 'earth' is not much different, being the abbreviated form of k (a) + s (a) + ma = by the earth the milk is produced (a passive sentence).

From the fossilised word phala 'fruit', par = pṛ 'to cross, spread', etc. may have been deduced. In Tamil it is palam.

---

1 At some period in the history of the ur-Sanskrit, k-ṣa or k-ṣi would have been a word for milk, and kṣī ra would have been a clause: milk comes out. Later, ksīra 'milk' was a new word. The acc. pl. form gās is the basis of the English calf through the Germanic source, because the first sound was devoiced and the last s turned into the fricative.

31
From the Indus Valley to Europe

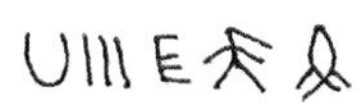

na dra-gha va-ga

The river will dry up. Irrigate (the lands).

The verbal form dra-gha (will dry up) has abbreviated as 'dry' in English, cognate with middle Dutch droghe, middle low German droge old Eng. dryga, German trocken. Even dragon is cognate with it, which was a mythical monster emitting-fire. The Eng. drought from the old Eng. drugath expresses the same dryness of weather.

In Sanskrit this dra-gha seems to be represented by the root drakh 'to be dry or arid'. In AV 11,7, 3d there is dra with vra. Before da (hill) and ra (fire) coalesced as the syllable dra, they formed a clause, meaning 'the hill burns' (= the land is extremely dry), later a phrase 'the dry land', even a 'desert'. Similarly, va (water) ra (speed) was a clause meaning 'the water flows', vra meaning 'a lake', later 'a swampy land'. Dra and vra oppose each other semantically. Dra may be a desert, vra may be a swamp. Dra is the first syllable of Dra-vi ḍa 'a hot country, or, the country of the hot sun'. The first syllable in vṛ -tra (who robs the heavenly waters is the reduced form of vra (swamp). The verse 'vraś ca draś cāpi śrīr mayi' means: Both the desert and the swamp are beauty in me (= make me beautiful).

It is remarkable that the verbal form dra-gha has travelled as far as Europe. na was extended as nada- m. nadī f. (river) in Vedic, but it has no trace in the cognate languages. The injunctive suffix –ga is still current in the rustic dialects of the Indian villages.

Dra may have been extended as drā (to run), daridrā (to wander), dru (to spread) in dru-ma (tree), even reduced to dṛ in dṛ-ti (leather).

32
The Ṛgveda X-106

The lowered status of the Aśvins

This hymn relating to Aśvins is very obscure. Geldner has left the stanzas 5-8 untranslated. The other stanzas too are not properly understood either by Sāyaṇa or by Geldner. The truth is that the twin-gods Aśvins have been grossly misunderstood as to their etymology and mythology. Even the background of the hymn is completely wrapped in darkness.

First of all, let us take up the problem of etymology. Because the assistance sought from them is available at short notice, the term Aśvin seems to be cognate with the adjective āśu 'quick, fast', also adv. 'soon, at once'. The verbal root is definitely aś, but it is the result of deduction from aś-va 'horse', the animal renowned as 'runner', which itself is the fossilised form of h̲a-ś-va of the ur-Sanskrit, an extension of the basic h̲a ['the neighing animal, producing an h-sound'] by śa (injury) and va (strength). The horse is etymologically 'an injurious and strong h-sound animal'. The meaning 'to run' 'hasten' has become inherently attached to it, as available in aś-vin. Even ś-van 'dog' is derived from this aś 'to run', but the radical a has been lost due to accent on the suffix. However, a of aś-vin has been retained due to some emphasis on its meaning, which may be 'hastener, reaching at short notice'. The word aś-vin is newly created from aś, and aś-va has evolved from h̲aśva. That is to say, aś-vin is directly derived from aś, not from aś-va.

The mythology of Aśvin is similarly obscure. Its conception is pre-Vedic. Aśvin was an official position in the pre-Vedic Indus society. It was the mature society of the urban Indus culture, speaking the inflexional form of the ur-Sanskrit. This official position had been created in the glorious days of the Indus civilisation for civil administration. They formed a two-man team of the rapid action force of the fire brigade. They were quick to render assistance even at short notice. The radical a was obstinately retained in the formation of the word, because it was newly created.

But their constant duality or association in pair was very remarkable and also the cause 'of some sarcasm or ridicule, which has culminated in the ideas contained in this hymn. There would have been even some other grounds for criticism. They had to do with wide range of activities, mainly of public interest, such as the duties of the municipal corporation. People were advised to contact them for any problem. Their most remarkable duty was perhaps the fire-fighting, which is natural in any urbanised society. Always carrying water in big vessels may have associated them with the water-buffaloes. Moving in pairs likened them to the two wings of a bird. Their selfless service in undertaking risky jobs likened them to the sacrificial animals. Their comparison with other animals is not happy. Their comparison with the biting serpents and the blades of a scissor is ironical. All the ridiculous comparisons may be seen in context of the texts and their translation. There is also some vague reference to the loose civil administration.

There are parallels in the linguistic and social history of mankind when a word of very good intention has undergone very drastic degradation in meaning, or when a social class of high status has suffered humiliation and downfall.

The word śūdra originally meant 'running (-dra) for the welfare of others (śu-). The śūdras were the respectable public servants of the ancient culture. At the zenith of its glory, it was the most sought after status, but some sort of excesses in their position might have reduced it to the fourth class of the Aryan social order.

Almost similar was the fate of the office of the Aśvins. Its constant two-ness accompanied by some other faults and excesses became the points of ridicule and criticism. When swung into action, they did not mind their car being drawn by asses and buffaloes, although usually their cars were drawn by horses. If we make a laughter of their good deeds, they may be summarised in this little hymn.

Even at the beginning of the medieval period in the Indian history, some professionally warrior clans, fighting with swords and arrows, became redundant after the development of the modern warfare technology. They had to adopt lower professions. Even when they claim to be Kshatriyas, they are rated as backward communities.

A few words about the language too have to be said. The words used in the present hymn belong to the lower middle class in the society. Though many of them are slangs, some appear to be the creation of the singer himself, betraying a modern outlook. They will be noticed in the individual stanzas. Many aspirates have to be explained through the corresponding unaspirates, and r through l. Some phonetic peculiarity of the hymn reflects in the modern vernaculars.

There has been an in-depth study of the Vedic language. But, thanks to some misconceptions in the reconstruction of the human history, specially with reference to India, the linguistic study has suffered. A special victim has been the Vedic lexicography. Every Vedic word is attempted to be derived from the Vedic roots and, when we try to go into a more ancient period, we are led to the lands outside India and to a language hardly anything like the ancestor of Sanskrit. Now we vehemently repudiate these ideas, because the obscure Vedic words go to the ruins of the Indus civilisation. Thus, to quote just a few: nag 'night' goes to the ur-Sanskrit clause ṇa ga = the light has gone away; ram 'ash' to ra ma = the fire has extinguished; ṛbīsa 'a cavity in the earth from which hot vapours arise' and vanád 'fire' to ra bī ṣu va ṇa ṭha = when the fire heated the water, in the dwelling the vapour circulated, etc. The Vedic is the later inflexional stage of the ur-Sanskrit, and the clauses quoted above are two stations before the Vedic, at the isolating stage. Several millenniums earlier, there was a society with this primitive language, but their material life had reached the dizzy heights, as we can imagine through the results of excavation.

Unless we take account of this ruined civilisation, we cannot interpret the Vedic texts. There is a continuity in the civilisation, in spite of wide gaps caused by the natural disasters.

While discussing this little hymn of the RV, we have to start from the Indus civilisation, when a human language was born, which was the isolating stage of the ur-Sanskrit. It passed on to the agglutinative stage and reached the inflexional stage, which culminated in the Vedic language. The language of the present hymn is almost on the last milestone of the Vedic language, just on the outer ring of the orthodox Vedic society. It relates to us the story of the bygone age. Through the language, we can imagine the state of the society.

The Aśvins, the officials of the Indus civil administration, at the decadent period, did not command as much respect as they had at the golden period of their history.

A way to go to the depth of the meaning of its stanzas is to pierce it through eyes - looking at it as if digging with a hoe. As the eyes penetrate the words, the mind joins it to make a hole to go deeper. The meaning seems sitting at the bottom. This extra-ordinary method connects a modern slang with the ancient one of the hymn.

The traditional etymology has little scope. The common sense often works wonderfully. Words are such as may give any relevant meaning, not imagined elsewhere.

In the family books of the RV, they are the most prominent gods after Indra, Agni and Soma, but in the later Hindu mythology they are almost forgotten. They are the Aśvinī-kumāras, the divine physicians, which hardly throws any light on their prestige among the orthodox singers of the RV.

In the following pages, each stanza of the hymn is followed by grammatical notes, literal translation and further explanation of the contents. As far as possible, the connection of a stanza with the following is shown, although, in many cases, they are unconnected, the reference to the Aśvins, however, being the main point.

1. ubhā u nūnáṃ tád íd arthayethe
   vítanvāthe dhíyo vástrāpáseva,
   sadhrīcīnā yātave prém ajīgaḥ
   sudíneva pṛ́kṣa ā taṃsayethe

Though dhī is generally said to mean 'thought', it is here 'activity', representing the verb dhā 'to do'. Apás, accented on the suffix, is the agent noun 'worker, artisan, weaver'; sadhrīcīna = sadhri + añc, the weak base sadhrīc making sadhrīcīnā meaning 'leaning towards each other, going hand in hand, collaborating'; pra + gṛ 'to ask for, order'; pra īm ajīgaḥ = One asked them; sudinā < su-din from dā 'to give', = liberal; pṛkṣas represents the root pṛc 'to mix, come in contact'. Thus it means 'friendship' ā + taṃs 'to decorate' figuratively means 'to welcome'.

Translation: Both of you certainly ask for that alone. You spread your activities like the weavers their cloths. They were asked to go to you collaborating with each other. As liberals you welcomed their friendship.

The Aśvins were supposed to attend to wide range of activities. But they are ridiculously compared to weavers. They walked hand in hand to help others. Therefore, many needy persons were advised to contact them for help, which they readily rendered. It is clear, they were certainly not 'horsemen' or any aspect of nature. They are the pre-historic human beings, holding some position of authority in the civil administration of the Indus society. 'That alone' may indirectly refer to 'bribe', which may be expected from the corrupt officials. The second verse of the stanza may suggest their hypocrisy.

2. uṣṭāreva phárvareṣu śrayethe
prāyogéva śvātryā śāsur éthaḥ,
dūtéva hí ṣṭho yaśásā jāneṣu
māpa sthātam mahiṣévávapānāt

Uṣṭar may be derived from ukṣ 'to moisten', and they may refer to 'turtle', which is called palvala-vāsa 'residing in pool'. Then pharvara also may be the dialectal form of palvala 'pool, pond', aspirated on the first syllable and undergoing rhotacism in case of l; prāyoga may be the creation of the present author from pra + ā + yuj meaning 'employee, official'. śvātryā is the inst. sg. form of śvātrī, being actually śva (dog) + ad (to eat) + tṛ + f. ī = śvāt-trī 'a female dog-eater'. śāsus from śās 'to rule' means 'office, order'; yaśás, accented on suffix, is an adj. meaning 'famous'. A buffalo likes remaining in waters because of its hot nature.

Translations: Like turtles you remain in pools of waters. As officials you come to the office with a female dog-eater. You are famous as messengers among the public. Like a buffalo do not stay out of pond.

Because the Aśvins were the men of the fire brigade, their office was stationed near a pool of waters. They always carried waters with them. They are ridiculed as remaining in waters like a turtle. They were probably attended by a woman of ill-repute, who accompanied them to the office. They are said to be renowned, because their duties pertained to public interest. But they are again ridiculed by their comparison with buffalo, always plunging in the pool of waters. Every sentence of praise is mixed with jokes amounting to insult.

Though they were professionally enjoined to help the public in distress and they deserved praise and reward, they are praised with ridiculous words. We can imagine the status of the Aśvins among the people of the lower middle class of the Vedic society.

3. sākaṃyújā śakunásyeva pakṣā
paśvéva citrā yájur ā gamiṣṭam,
agnír iva devayór dīdivāṃsā
párijmāneva yajathaḥ purutra.

paśvā = pasv-au for paśū (dual). citra from cit meaning 'living, alive'. yajus = sacrifice, worship. Perhaps some work of public interest is intended. deva-yu = devoted to god, god-worshipper. pari-jman = pari-aj-man = the wandering priest. yaj (to worship) really means: to do some work of public interest.

Translation: Joined together like the wings of a bird, come to our sacrifice like living sacrificial animals. Shining like the fire of a god-worshipper, like the wandering priests, you do your work at many places.

These Aśvins always operated in pairs, but the comparison with the wings of a bird is not an appreciation. Sometimes, they had to undertake risky jobs. There is a veiled praise and ridicule for this when they are asked to come to the sacrifice like living animals, only to be killed.

4. āpī vo asmé pitáreva putrā
úgreva rucā nṛpátīva turyái,
íryeva puṣṭyai kiraneva bhujyai
śruṣṭīvāneva havam ā gamiṣṭam

āpi from āp 'to arrive, reach' in dual suggests arrival in 'pairs'. Therefore, āpi = pair. If ugra = strong, ruca may mean 'weak'. Similarly, turī in opposition to nṛpati 'king' may mean 'needy, distressed', iryā in opposition to puṣṭi 'health' may be 'food'. kiraṇa 'rays' suggests that bhuji is 'earth' on which the rays fall. śruṣṭi is an extension of śruṣ, the contracted form of śravas from śru 'to hear'. Or, śruṣ-ṭi can directly be connected with śru through an interposed -s-. śruśṭī-van is 'one who is quick to hear the distress call'.

Translation: Your pair is to us like parents to children, like strong men to weak ones, like kings to needy persons, like food for health, like the rays (of the sun) to the earth. Come to our call as one who is quick to hear a distress-call.

Sometimes the etymology cuts sorry figure in reaching the intended meaning. Thus ruca cannot convey the meaning 'weak' etymologically. But, if ruca has anyhow some connection with arc 'to pray' through ṛc, it may indicate 'one who prays, asks for help'. turī 'needy' may reflect in ā-tura 'distressed'.

The stanzas 5 and 6 make syntactically one unit, the 6 d connecting all the pādas.

5. váṃsageva pūṣaryā śimbātā
mitréva ṛtā śātárā śātapantā
vājevoccā váyasā gharmyeṣṭhā
méseveṣā saparyā púrīṣā

Because the pāda c has vāja 'horse' and d has meṣa 'ram', vaṃsaga in the pāda a may be a 'bull', as suggested by Sāyaṇa: The basic vṛṣan has been extended as vṛṣa-ka, prakritised as vasaka and further corrupted as vaṃsaga by an anusvāra on the first syllable and voicing on the last syllable. The other words of this stanza have the colour of a slang. pūṣan from puṣ 'to nourish' has undergone rhotacism in pūṣarya to suggest unhealthy state of nourishment, resulting in corpulence, reinforced by śimbāta 'pod-shaped'. śatara comes from the same root as śat-ru 'enemy' and has the adjectival meaning. But śāta-panta is contrary, meaning 'protecting (pā) from 'injury' (śāta). vayas may suggest the 'speed' of the bird. purīṣa 'faeces' has been used adjectively, meaning 'foul-smelling'. saparya 'adorable' seems to have a perverted sense like pūṣarya, namely 'mischievous'. Colloquially, even a word of good intention is used in the opposite sense. Though iṣa means 'strong', it may suggest 'bluntness'.

Translation: Corpulent and pod-shaped like bulls; true, injurious and protector like friends; elevated, bird-like and perspiring like horses; blunt, mischievous and foul-smelling like rams.....

Corpulence and pod-shapedness are not good signs for a bull, and when Aśvins are compared with it, they are more ridiculed than praised. If said to be friends, the adjectives are not matching. A comparison with horses is tolerable, but the same with a ram is repugnant. Even the editors of the pada-text were not familiar with the slangs. Therefore, they did not try to analyse them.

6. sṛ́ṇyeva jarbhárī turphárītū
naitośéva turphárī parpharīkā,
udanyajéva jémanā maderū
tā me jarāyu ajáram marāyu.

sṛṇya, derived from sṛ 'to creep', is cognate with sarpa 'serpent', jarbhari = *jar-hvari from hvar/hvṛ 'to be crooked'. Cf. Hindi jībh from jihvā 'tongue'. turpharītu = tvar (hastily) + pharītu (injuring) from pṛt/part 'to injure', the radical p aspirated due to the preceding r and the suffix -u added with an interposed -ī-. naitośa 'the blades of a scissor' has very distant connection with tud 'to afflict'. turphari = *tṛp-ri from tṛp/turp, the radical p aspirated due to the preceding r, the suffixal -ri itself dissolved as -ari. This tṛp is cognate with dṛbh in darbha 'a pricking grass'. parpharīka 'uniting frequently' is derived from pṛc/park, the radical p aspirated due to the preceding r, the suffix -a added with an interposed -ī-. udan-ya from udan 'water' takes -ja (born) probably to mean 'fermented in water'. jeman 'food' may be traced to the colloquial jim 'to eat', and this 'food' is probably the 'cooked rice', which becomes intoxicating if fermented in water. Jarāyu, finally shortened due to the following vowel in ajaram, used adverbially, marāyu also shortened finally to rhyme with jarāyu.

Translation: Extremely crooked and biting hastily like serpents; pricking sharply and uniting repeatedly like (the blades of) a scissor; intoxicating like boiled rice fermented in water. These two, (although) destined to grow old and die, may be unaging for me.

The Aśvins are praised and criticised at the same time. A comparison with the crooked serpent is disparaging, but the suggested punishment inflicted by them on criminals is praised. The comparison with the blades of scissors has both undertones. They always work in unity by coming together like the blades of a scissor. The third verse is a veiled criticism of their drunkardness, but there is praise for their tireless work. The last verse is a blessing: they are desired to remain active like a young man. This is a rare or perhaps the only stanza in which the singer appears to bless the divine being. This also shows that this Vedic deity, at least, was a social figure of a bygone age.

The 7th and 8th stanzas refer to two different incidents. The 7th recounts the case of a murder.

7. pajréva cárcaraṃ jāraṃ marāyu
kṣádmevārtheṣu tartarītha ugrā,
ṛbhū nāpat kharamajrā kharájrur
vāyúr ṇá parpharat kṣayad rayīṇām.

pajra is cognate with the controversial pājas 'side, as seen from the front', with bāhu 'arm', the colloquial pā̃jā 'the distance between the two arms', pā̃jrā 'side', and means 'breast'. It is the metaphorical subject of the verb 'kill' expressed adverbially through an adjective (marāyu 'mortal' > acted mortally = killed), the object being jāra 'paramour'. In this connection, iva is the conjunction 'when'. pajra 'breast' stands for the 'harlot' herself.

In the second verse, ugrā (0 brave ones!) brings Aśvins pronominally as subject of the intensive verb tar-tar 'to scale, mount', having some twin-building suggested by the breasts as object. Even kṣadman 'knife' is the subject of the same verb meaning 'to descend'. The verb is in the present tense to present a vivid description of the incident.

The second hemistich continues the story. kharajru is a slang and, though not analysed in the pada-text, may be analysed as khara + jru. Here jru is the abbreviated form of jāru = jāra, and khara stands for khalā (a flirt woman). khara-jru is just another paramour, attached with the same harlot. Though kharamajrā also is not analysed in the pada-text; it may be analysed as khara + majra. The latter is an agent noun from majj 'to dive, plunge into water', and khara = an ass. Just after plunging into water, the ass begins to roll on the earth in dust, and its bath becomes meaningless, khara-majra is the adjective of ṛbhu 'the carpenter, architect, engineer'. He works perspiringly and gets tired, then takes a bath and rest, but begins working to perspire again. Thus he behaves like an ass.

The particle na is conjunction 'when' here. Colloquially, na is used as such even now in dialects.

parpharat is the intensive form of pṛ in past tense, aspirated on the radical syllable on account of the preceding r, meaning 'to scatter'. Both parpharat and kṣayad govern the object rayi in genitive.

Translation: When the breasts (= harlot) acted mortally towards (= killed) the frequenting paramour, o brave ones: (you) scaled (the twin-building and descended) like a knife on the treasures. When the (second) paramour came to the architect bathed like an ass, he scattered (and) destroyed his property like storm.

This stanza, full of slangs and distorted grammar and syntax, seems to give a scrappy account of the murder of a rich paramour, who used to visit a harlot, suggested by the breasts acting mortally. The same breasts suggest the existence of a twin-building, where the paramours lived. Perhaps the architect had confided the building plan and the position of the strong room to Aśvins who took control of the treasures. This infuriated the second paramour who ransacked the home of the architect.

Though an ancient poetry, this stanza has a modern outlook. The ruins of the Indus civilisation suggest such state of affairs.

The 8th stanza refers to a rescue operation, which was not properly handled.

8. gharméva mádhu jaṭháre sanérū
Bháge 'vitā turphári phārivāram,
pataréva cácarā candrá-nirniṅ
mana-ṛṅgā mananyā ná jágmī

saneru is perhaps derived from sana 'old' and means 'useless, in bad condition'. It qualifies gharma 'cauldron', the vessel fetching water to the site of disaster. phāriva 'ploughshare' is derived from the verb pṛ 'to spread' extended by a prefixed s, spṛ meaning 'to split', but the prefixed s was lost after aspirating the radical p. bhaga 'furrow' is the result of splitting through the ploughshare. With its loc. sg. form bhaga is compounded with avitā from av (for the regular ūta). Both patara and cacara are dialectal forms, the former for patra 'leaf' meaning 'lean and thin, emaciated', and the latter derived from car 'to serve', meaning 'a serving disciple', later becoming celā in vernaculars. Candra-nirṇij 'having a shining or white cloth' has been used adverbially. The last pāda has three adjectives, qualifying celā.

Translation: The old cauldrons were like honey in the stomach. The scratching ploughshares were protected well in the furrow. The emaciated disciples in white cloths were active as well as jovial and mindful.

The old cauldron perhaps refers to the outdated equipments used by the team of the fire brigade. All the waters leaked out before they were carried to the site of disaster. The 'honey in stomach' may be an apt ancient proverb and ridicules the uselessness of a misplaced effort. The 'scratching ploughshare protected in furrow' perhaps points to some equipment hardly brought in use or to the lethargic workers not going to the site of disaster. It may also have some obscene conotation. The emaciated disciples in white cloths' may refer to the low-paid attendants of the fire brigade, but they are praised to be active, jovial and mindful in their duties.

At the end of the stanza, we come to realise that the situation could not be brought under control on account of various deficiencies. Whatever was achieved was due to the low-paid workers.

The 9th stanza is an advisory to the team of the Aśvins.

9. bṛhanteva gambháreṣu pratiṣṭhām
pādeva gādhaṃ tárate vidāthaḥ,
kárṇeva śasur ánu hí smárātho
áṃśeva no bhajatáṃ citrám ápnaḥ.

The use of the verb vid 'to know' and anu-smṛ 'to listen to, obey' in subjunctive by the singer for Aśvins does not appear to accord with their old status. It looks like somebody advising his subordinate staff towards their duties. Then it means that by that time the Aśvins had lost much of their prestige as deity and they were slightly above the common man. karṇa 'ear' really stands for the subordinate staff. aṃśa 'part, share' is a 'position' in business and means a 'share-holder or sharer'. apnas is derived from āp 'to get' through the irregular present base ap-n- meaning 'profit'. citra = due, proper.

Translation: (As officials of the civil administration) You should know the status (of the common man) like tall men in ditches; (you should know) the depth (of water) like the legs of the swimmer; you should listen to the order like the subordinate staff; like sharer give us our due profit.

As we go through the translation of the stanza in a free style, we feel that it relates to the day-to-day affairs of the society. A social life comprises rich and poor (tall men and ditch), profiteers and losers (swimmers), and there are problems of insubordination and cooperation. It is the right of the investors to demand due profit from the sharers.

The 10th stanza points to the corrupt administration.

10. āraṅgaréva mádhvérayethe
sāraghéva gávi nīcīnábāre,
kināreva svédam āsisvidānā
ksāmevorjā suyavasāt sacethe.

Whatever the etymology, āraṅgara is a 'bee', because it is connected with honey. The first element of the word reflects in ali 'bee'. The final element -gara too seems to be connected with 'humming' (gṛ). ā + īr means 'to bring'. sāragha is a special kind of fly, colloquially called 'kukur-māchi', generally found on the body of the bovine cattle and on dogs. bāra is the modern colloquial 'bār/bāl' (hair), generally low-lying as on dogs and bovine cattle. Thus, ni + añc > nyañc, weak base nīc- makes nīcīna = low-lying. kināra is the insect born out of foul-smelling sweat sticking to the inner garments of dirty workers, generally called 'cillar'. The word kināra (= kinnar) itself would have phonetically turned into cillar through initial palatalisation and change of n into l. ā-sisvid-āna is perhaps the colloquial form of ā-sasvad-āna from svad 'to enjoy' with some distortion in meaning. ūrjā is the inst. sg. form of ūrj 'strength'. ṣu-yavasa+ad (eating good grass) has been used as adv. of manner.

Translation: You produce honey like bees; (lie) like flies on the bull having low-lying hairs. Sucking sweat like 'cillar' you bestow strength upon emaciated (animals), as if they eat good grass.

All clauses of this stanza appear to have metaphorical meanings: they say something and mean something else.

Though full of slangs, this stanza has given us no trouble. In Ragh. 2,5 Kālidāsa speaks of the fly falling on cow as daṃśa, but sāragha is a dialectal or even rustic word. This stanza wants to expose some evils of Aśvins. Perhaps those officials of the ancient society accumulated wealth through evil means, not only from the rich but also from the poor citizens. But they also helped the poor from this wrongly accumulated wealth. In each case, the comparison is subtly metaphorical.

11. ṛdhyāma stómaṃ sanuyāma vājam
ā no mántram saráthehópa yātam
yáśo ná pakváṃ mádhu góṣvantar
ā bhūtāṃśo aśvinoḥ kāmam aprāḥ

Translation: Let us multiply the prayer (and) get wealth. Come to our invitation in your car here. There is rich fame like honey in songs. Let Bhūtāṃśa fulfil the desire of Aśvins.

33
Origins of Speech (RV 10,71)

Geldner rightly says that the 10th cycle of the RV is 'the big appendix' to the kernel consisting of the 'family books' (RV II-VII), the smaller appendices being I (in two parts) and VIII. Its subject-matter is not the gods and sacrifices of the early books of the RV. It deals with secular matters and the ordinary events of the Vedic society, recorded by the lesser talented poets. But, because these were the ancient records of the ancestors in the eyes of the redactors of the Saṃhitā texts, they were included in the compilation. The subject-matter is varied in nature, some of them being very obscure, even difficult to be headlined.

The origin of speech is considered to be a modern speculation. It was started in the 19th century, but soon it was abandoned after some wild speculations. The German linguist Wilhelm von Humboldt proposed the typological classification of languages as isolating, agglutinative and inflexional, which gives some hint about the beginning of the human speech. But it is no more seriously discussed now.

In India, there had been a tradition of linguistic analysis, but it was restricted to Sanskrit. The typological classification of languages is a modern concept, and the Sanskrit grammarians never visualised it. The pioneers of the linguistic analysis in India were the gods like Brahmā, Bṛhaspati and Indra in succession. But the RV 10,71 seems to be concerned with the origin of the human speech. The Vedic singers outside the sphere of the family books were somehow aware of the early form of the Vedic language, because their outlook was secular and their reach was far beyond the sacrificial activities. In the 10th cycle of the RV, we appear to move among the people who were not much different from those of the AV. They form a class of people midway between the priests of the RV and the men on street of the AV. They hardly talk about sacrifices, and the gods they talk of are not exactly the same as described in the family books. Agni is not the same Purohita as at the beginning of the RV, and Indra is not the same ferocious fighter, and so on. They take note of the worldly vices and virtues of the ordinary public life. It is only the language which is, more or less, antiquated like the Vedic.

To go even beyond their speculation on modern lines, we may start with the human beings walking erect and their tongue getting away from the larynx, so that the prolonged cry of the horizontally walking animals broke into syllables. When the cry was monosyllabic, it was an order. Otherwise, there were bisyllabic or trisyllabic clauses in the indicative mood. It is from here that these late Vedic singers appear to say something. Of course, their statement is scrappy. The opening stanzas hastily reach the Vedic stage, which too was already antiquated for them.

The first stanza opens with address to Bṛahaspati, the god of speech, who is said to have learnt grammar from Brahmā and imparted it to Indra. The subject of the verb pra-īr 'to utter' is suppressed, who must be the primitive speakers of the language. The phrase nāma-dheyaṃ dadhānaḥ (giving names) points to the naming of syllables ka, kha, etc. one by one. Some were phonemes, some were just allophones of certain phonemes. Some were likely to be ignored. Freely translated, the first stanza says:

1. O Bṛhaspati, first of all, the original elements of the speech (the phonemes), which (the primitive human beings) uttered, naming them (individually), were born. What was excellent and phonemic among them, kept lovingly in hiding, came out.
   bṛhaspate prathamaṃ vāco agraṃ yat prairata nāmadheyaṃ dadhānaḥ,
   yad eṣāṃ śreṣṭhaṃ yad aripram āsīt prenā tad eṣāṃ nihitaṃ guhāviḥ.

It was the isolating stage of the language. It moved instinctively like the early creatures of the creation. Gradually, the grammar began to evolve. It was its mind. Then it began to move as desired by the speakers. It was the agglutinative stage.

The word sakhi and its derivative sakhya refer to those involved in speech and their action. The second stanza tells something about the language proceeding from the agglutinative to the inflexional stage.

2. saktum iva titaūnā punanto yatra dhīrā manasā vācam akrata,
   atra sakhāyaḥ, sakhyāni jānate bhadraiṣāṃ lakṣmīr nihitādhi vāci.

As the wisemen mentally fashioned the speech, as if purifying the groats in a sieve, the intelligent people knew the secret of speech. Its profound beauty is concealed in its grammar.

At the inflexional stage, the language branched into several dialects. Very thoughtful ideas began to come out. The word, yajña (sacrifice) stands for the 'careful labour' applied to the beautification of the language. The singers composed hymns in several metres. The absolutive form ā-bhṛ-tya (having decorated, ornamented) stands for its diversification in different dialects. The third stanza seems to suggest the beginning of the composition of the Vedic hymns.

3. yajñena vācaḥ padavīyam āyan tām anvavindann ṛṣiṣu praviṣṭām
   tām ābhṛtya vyadadhuḥ purutrā tāṃ sapta rebhā abhi saṃ navante

Through a careful labour the language was brought to elegance. The people found it entering the singers. They spread it (as dialects) to different places. Seven birds (metres) accompany it.

The fourth stanza speaks enigmatically. Does it refer to the Indus texts, which was partly lost and partly gone into the hands of the Tantrics? From the study of the Āgama literature, it appears that they had failed to read and understand the antiquated Indus texts, but their attempt to decode them gave rise to the disciplines of Āgama, Tantra and Mantra. Then they began to form a sectarian literature, which was comprehensible to a few people. Because the monosyllabic words had mostly disappeared from the language, these sectarian people began to see the gods, stars and planets in the syllabic symbols.

4. uta tvaḥ paśyaḥ na dadarśa vācam uta tvaḥ śṛṇvan ṇa śṛṇoty enām,
   uto tvasmai tanvaṃ vi sasre jāyeva patya uśatī suvāsāḥ.

And some one, even though looking at it, does not see it. And some one, even though listening to it, does not understand it. On the other hand, to someone it exposes its body like a loving, well-dressed wife to her husband.

Later, many heretics appeared in the society, who had visited substandard schools of learning and were not properly educated. The fifth stanza is full of slangs.

The phrase sthira-pīta (having stagnant drink) in sakhya (friendship) may be freely translated as 'one fossilised in learning'. He does not want to learn anything new and sticks to his own viewpoint obstinately. The word vājina is not derived from vāc, as explained through Pāṇini's ayasmayādīni cchandasi. It is derived from vāja (booty, wealth), as ajina (skin) from aja (goat). It means 'contest for prize'. Similarly, dhenu stands for dhenā (speech), and adhenvā means 'speechlessly, like a dumb'. It seems, even the Vedic language was becoming antiquated. Those who understood it even partly did not want to listen to others.

5. uta tvaṃ sakhye sthira-pītam āhur nainaṃ hinvantyapi vājineṣu,
adhenvā carati māyayaiṣa vācaṃ śuśruvāṃ aphalām apuṣpām

Someone is fossilised in learning. He is not, therefore, sent to elocution contest. Having heard fruitless and flowerless speech, he moves like a dumb, feigning scholarship.

The poet does not hide the treachery and unfaithfulness in scholarship, which might have been prevalent in the society. The term saci-vid is intentionally not very different from saciva (advisor, counsellor). He is one who has been trained in many subjects. Even bhāga is 'sharing knowledge' with others, and alaka is a prākritism for arka (song, praise) from ṛc 'to sing' and means a 'distorted speech'.

6. yas tityāja sacividam sakhāyaṃ na tasya vācyapi bhāgo asti,
yad im śṛṇoty alakaṃ śṛṇoti na hi pra veda sukṛtasya panthām.

If someone has deserted his comrade of wide knowledge, there is no addition to his knowledge. Whatever one hears from him is a distorted speech. He does not know the way of a good deed.

The classical poet Bhavabhūti has said that the teacher imparts knowledge equally to a dull and an intelligent student. But there is a great difference in reception. The seventh stanza tells the same thing in a roundabout way. The term mano-java (the speed of mind) refers to 'intelligence'. The second hemistich says that the learning is like a pond. For some student it is too deep. For some others it is not so, but he does not take the full advantage of the bath. But some students have comfortable bath in the pond of learning, so that he gets the title of susnāta or snātaka (a learned graduate).

7. akṣaṇvantaḥ karṇavantaḥ sakhāyo manojaveṣu asamā babhūvuḥ
adaghnāsa upakakṣāsa u tve hradā snātvā u tve dadṛśre

Learners having (similar) eyes and ears are unequal in intelligence. Some are seen to have plunged either face-deep or arm-deep in the pool (of learning), while some others are seen having comfortable bath.

The students working together in collaboration have often desire for individual's excellence. Thus they become divided in heart and the zeal for work is reduced. Some are diligent, others are not so. The words of the eighth stanza are slangs, not in conformity with the standard usage. Therefore, we may take liberty in translation too. Oha-brahman (whose poetry is burden-like) stands for a 'laboured poet'. He has no poetic genius. But he also deserts his comrades.

8. hṛdā taṣṭeṣu manaso javeṣu yad brahmaṇā saṃ yajante sakhāyaḥ,
atrāha tvaṃ vi jahur vedyābhir oha-brahmāṇo vi caranty u tve.

While Brahmins sacrifice together as comrades, their intention split in heart, the laboured poets desert their intelligent partners and go away with little knowledge.

The contents of the last three stanzas are not clear. They try to report the sorry state of affairs of some academic institutions and pupils of that time. There were some substandard academic institutions, and their products too were substandard, doing nothing but claiming more than what they were worthy of. However, some of them were decidedly of good quality.

There were two types of comrades, those who stayed with the team, and those who left it. Those who went away were called non-creative (a-pra-jajñi from jan). Their language had dialectal overtones. A Brāhmaṇa is one who knows the Brahman (prayer), but a sute-kara is a do-nothing fellow. The word siri is derived from the colloquial *sir, reflecting in the Hindi verb sil-nā 'to sew'. Therefore, siri may be a thread.

9. ime ye nārvāṅ na paraś caranti na brāhmaṇāso na sutekarāsaḥ,
ta ete vācam abhi-padya pāpayā sirīs tantram tanvate apraja -jñayaḥ.

Those who neither go away nor stay near are neither academicians nor labourers. They afflict the sacred speech with profane (speech). These non-creative labourers turn threads into cloths.

Till recently in Indian academic institutions, the students were sent up for final examination. Some of them were also withheld due to their poor performance. The tenth stanza refers to almost similar state of affairs in ancient times. The sent up students were praised.

10. sarve nandanti yasasāgatena sabhāsāhena sakhyā sakhāyaḥ,
kilviṣa-spṛt pitu-ṣaṇir hy eṣām araṃ hito bhavati vājināya.

All friends rejoice over the friend who has come with fame by contesting in the assembly. He removes blemishes. He procures food. He is capable to contest for prize when sent up.

The last stanza of this hymn states some bare facts, but it has suggestions for many things. This is perhaps the only hymn in the whole RV which scrappily intends to say something on the origin of a language.

With the application of our own reasoning about the popular literary activities in an enlightened society, we may imagine that poems were composed even outside the Saṃhitā collection, though they were hardly taken note of. The Vedic language was proceeding towards the classical stage, and the language of the transitional period mostly remains unrecorded. Even when the people were speaking the early form of the modern vernaculars in India, the poets used to write their poems in the outdated Apabhraṃśa. Similarly, by the time of the 10th cycle of the RV, the Vedic language was on the threshold of the classical stage. But the lesser talented popular poets used to write their poems in the slightly outdated Vedic language, as we can imagine from the language of the khila-sūktas.

We suppose, the first verse of the last stanza refers to this activity. Those who could not compose poems of the old standard just recited them. The beginning of the Brāhmaṇa literature was on the threshold.

> 11. ṛcāṃ tvaḥ poṣam āste pupuṣvān gāyatraṃ tvo gāyati śakvarīṣu, brahmā tvo vadati jāta-vidyāṃ yajñasya mātrām vi mimīta u tvaḥ.

Someone (of the RV tradition) makes addition in the ṛk-verses; someone (of the SV tradition) sings in śakvarī metres; someone (of the AV tradition) speaks the maternity science; and someone (of the YV tradition) measures the extent of sacrifice.

34
The Words of the Indus Culture in the Atharvaveda

At the isolating stage of the ur-Sanskrit, we envisage only a monosyllabic vocabulary. It consisted of 34 consonants followed by 14 vowels, briefly mentioned in the Māheśvara-sūtras at the beginning of the Pāṇini's grammar. The 14 vowels themselves were a part of the vocabulary. We assume that there were 34 × 14 = 476 consonantal syllables, besides the 14 vowels. Some stops too were ligatured with the nasals m n, semivowels y r l v and sibilants ś ṣ s. Thus the total vocabulary would have amounted to 1000 monosyllabic words, more or less. They were gradually ousted from the language as it reached the inflexional stage, but the traditional Sanskrit lexicographers hastened to record them, as we see them compiled in the modern Sanskrit dictionaries. Some monosyllabic words like hrī, ṣrī, etc. are still used in Sanskrit, while some of them were retained by extending them on either side; e.g. tma was extended as tma-n and ā-tma-n.

Two monosyllabic words, vra and dra, recorded in the AV 11,7,3 are still obscure. The traditional lexicographers inform that va = water, da = hill, ra = fire, speed. Getting some hints from them, we suppose that va ra and da ra were clauses: va ra = the water flows; da ra = the sand is hot. Through the phrase 'the flowing water', we have some words like vār, vāri (water). Even the phrase 'the hot sand' has fossilised as adri (stone), darī (cave), the verb dṛ (to split).

We suppose that vra, contracted from va ra, referring to the region of the flowing waters, means 'swamp', and dra, contracted from da ra, referring to the region of the hot sands, means 'desert'. Thus vraś ca draś cāpi śrīr mayi (AV 11,7,3) seems to mean: Both swamp and desert are beauty in me.

The question is: who is this *man* referred to by *mayi*?

This verse forms a part of the hymn called uc-chiṣṭa brahma. Here the participle uc-chiṣṭa has not been correctly understood by the scholars. Though -śiṣṭa is evidently derived from śiṣ (to be left out), it is more probably a secondary root, the weakened form of the verb śās 'to teach, instruct, rule over'. From the original form of the verb we have śāstā 'teacher', and from the weak form of the verb we have śiṣ-ya 'pupil', śiṣṭa 'cultured', the desiderative form śikṣate (learns) for *śiśikṣate (lit. desires to be instructed).

In this connection, we may refer to ud + śās in: nu me brahmāṇy agna uc-chaśādhi (RV 7,1,20 a). Geldner has translated it thus: Now teach us rightly the devotional prayers, O Agni.

The participle uc-chiṣṭa then here means: rightly taught, rightly instructed, and the person taught is the singer himself, because the pronominal form me (RV 7,1,20) refers to the same man as mayi (AV 11,7,3).

Thus the AV-passage clearly says: the swamp and desert are beauty in me, the singer. That is to say, both swamp and desert are agreeable to the singer. But the swamp and desert are just symbolic here. The one, cold or damp, and the other, hot or dry, refer to the two extremes of quality in a thing. If a prayer has been devotionally addressed, its outer form, good or bad, is irrelevant.

We mark a difference of taste between the singers of the RV and AV. The former wants to be a true poet and the latter has no regard for a good poetry.

Though both swamp and desert are unpleasant places, the singer of the AV revels in them, as if they were beautiful places. The RVedic singers were materialists, while the AVedic singers were stoics.

The rightly instructed singer (ucchiṣṭa brahmā) of the AV says: For me everything is beautiful, whether it is the swampy land or the burning desert, because I have absorbed everything in myself.

35
Niṣṭhā

ni ṣa, ni ni ni ṣa-ṭha

The reading of these two almost identical texts may be doubtless. In the first case, the subject is in sg. and the verb is in the present tense. In the second case, the subject is in pl. and the same verb is having the past affix. How the sounds acquired meanings in a primitive language is only imaginable. Nothing can be said definitely.

The sound n came to be connected with the 'shining', 'flowing' aspect of some liquid. In some of the occurrences, na means a 'river'. We have nada in Sanskrit, which literally means 'flows and makes indistinct noise', referring to a small noisy river, from which a verb nad 'avyakte śabde' has been deduced in Sanskrit. We have elsewhere met with na ra meaning 'the river has begun flowing', which has fossilised as nālā 'a small water-channel'. Nīra 'water' also represents an original clause nī ra 'the water flows'. Ni too may refer to some 'shining liquid'. The clause ni ṣa perhaps means: the shining liquid comes out.

The Vedic language is vaguely thousands of years apart from its ur-stage, and the development of the meaning is not exactly known. A whole clause has turned into a preposition whose sole function is to lead the original meaning of the verb anywhere.

The clause ni ni ni ṣa-ṭha is a little extended: the subject in pl. and the verb in the past tense. The pl. noun ni 'the shining liquids' probably refers to the 'animal seed for procreation'. Then the past verb ṣa-ṭha perhaps means 'came out, was ejected'. The final part of the clause, namely ni ṣa-ṭha has fossilised as niṣṭhā in the RV, which should literally mean 'the ejected animal seed'. But it was analysed as nis-sthā by the editors of the pada-text, leading to other deviating meanings.

The word niṣṭhā occurs twice in the RV.

3,31,10 sampaśyamānā amadann abhi svaṃ
payaḥ pratnasya retaso dughānāḥ,
vi rodasī atapad ghoṣa eṣāṃ
jāte niṣṭhām adadhur goṣu vīrān.

In the verse d jāta seems to contrast with go, and niṣṭhā with vīra: they put niṣṭhā in jāta, vīras in go. If jāta (born) is the young cow, go may be the (barren) old cow. If niṣṭhā is the animal seed, vīra may be the cow-boy (in-charge of the barren old cows). Then we come to the following possible meaning:

They cheered up (abhi+amadan) seeing together (sam-paśyamānāḥ) the wealth, taking out milk from the old seed (= the older generation of the cows). Their cry heated the two worlds. They got the young cows impregnated and the old barren cows were put in charge of the cow-boys.

The multiplying of the wealth of cows is expressed in a refined language and the fate of the barren cows is mildly ignored.

Niṣṭhā occurs once more in 9, 110, 9:

adha yad ime pavamāna rodasī
imā ca viśvā bhuvanābhi majmanā,
yūthe ṇa niṣṭhā vṛṣabho vi tiṣṭhase.

Because the verb vi tiṣṭhase is intransitive, niṣṭhā is here an adjective, qualifying vṛṣabha with some necessary transfer of meaning. It means 'having animal seed, virile'.

Translation: When, then, O Pavamāna, you surpass (abhi tiṣṭhase) these two worlds and all these beings in greatness, you stand (vi tiṣṭhase) like a virile bull in the herd (of cows).

We see how the pre-historic phrase ni-ṣa-ṭha (the ejected shining liquid) was admitted in the Vedic vocabulary as niṣṭhā (the animal seed). It was already misunderstood by the editors of the pada-text (nis-sthā) on account of which it suffered drastic change in meaning.

36
Epilogue

The meaning of kucará

Pāṇini refers to -cara as a secondary suffix in the sense of 'former' (P. 5, 3, 53). Because car 'to go' is a verb from the oldest period of the Sanskrit language, the Rgvedic kucara and the classical gocara, in spite of their doubtful meanings, are associated with this verb.

The modern scholars, though convinced that the inflexional Sanskrit should have been preceded by the agglutinative ur-Sanskrit, fail to recognise that cara itself was a pluperfect form, ca 'to take place, be' + ra (the pluperfect affix), meaning 'had been' in the pre-historic period. Then ku-cara may be the later Vedic pluperfect from ku 'to roar' meaning 'had roared', ultimately becoming the adjective 'roaring'.[1] Also meaning, alternatively, 'had been on the earth', adj. 'roaming'.

Similarly, go-cara is the pluperfect from go-, meaning had gone into, adj. 'going into': dṛṣṭi-gocara 'visible', karṇa-gocara 'audible'.

We may also assume that co-ra is the ur-Sanskrit plupf. form from co- 'to steal', gho-ra from gho- 'to thunder'.

Then: pra tad viṣṇuḥ stavate viryeṇa mṛgo ṇa bhīmaḥ kucaro giri-ṣṭhāṇ = Viṣṇu is lauded for his strength like the mountain-dwelling, ferociously roaring (or roaming) bull.

Through the arrogant mischief of the so-called enlightened scholars the true Indian history has been effaced and blurred to such an extent that it will require centuries of labour to make it readable.

---

[1] Ku is dead as a verb in actual use, but kavi 'poet' is derived from it, and ghus 'say loudly', gā 'sing' are cognate with it. It also means 'earth', and may be in the oblique case.